The Agony

The Agony of Ecstasy

Olivia Gordon

continuum
LONDON • NEW YORK

Continuum

The Tower Building	15 East 26th Street
11 York Road	New York
London SE1 7NX	NY 10010

www.continuumbooks.com

First published 2004

British Library Cataloguing-in-Publication Data
A catalogue record for this book is available from the British Library.

ISBN 0–8264–6821–7 PB

Typeset by RefineCatch Limited, Bungay, Suffolk
Printed and bound by MPG Books Ltd, Bodmin, Cornwall

Acknowledgements

This book was one I always longed to write, and often attempted, but without the encouragement and generosity of four people, and the chain of events they put in motion, it would never have been set on the tenuous road to publication. It was Nicola Jeal who first offered to help me into print and leapt on my idea to write about ecstasy and depression, Liz Jones at the *Evening Standard* who printed my article on the subject, Mark Bostridge who read the article and saw the potential for a book, and Robin Baird-Smith, my publisher, who signed me up to write it and guided the publication with all his talent. A fifth person, who inspired me, taught me, gave me invaluable advice and was my personal proofreader as I drafted the book, was my mother. I thank these five people above all.

I am so grateful also for the expert guidance of my agent, Amanda Preston, the rest of the team at Continuum, Pamela Norris and Hilary Laurie. My deepest thanks go to my old friends, who have allowed me to base characters upon them; to David, my newer friends and random strangers, who have given me their enthusiasm; and to my dad, Anna and Aunt Naomi, who believed in me.

Acknowledgements

This book is based on true experience, but all names except my own have been changed, and many characters, details and scenes have been fictitiously created.

'Irreverence, challenge –
The end is misery.
Accept, and nothing can touch you . . .
Dance is law,
And all must celebrate.'

Euripides, Bacchae

Part One

Chapter One

'Don't think about it, just do it.' Through the hordes, in a rush, with a purpose, a young woman marches, almost dances. The advertisements are seen and avoided. Men and women's eyes meet, assess, flirt or reject. London is a mirror. Today success, yesterday abjection. Every morning she has to take the test. In the freshness of the day, all is newly prepared – sometimes it goes wrong. Every evening, the test takes longer and she is a survivor – proud, carefree when winning, contemptuous when losing. This is where the ego is refined, down here in the closed world, with trance music on a Walkman and artificial unflattering light. 'Beauty is the man in me – and feminism just an ugly woman,' she thinks.

What follows is the truth. It would be easier to write if I could call it fiction. If this book is categorized as fact, I am accountable; it is a real person the reader will judge. If you like, you can attribute to me the self-pitying foolishness of a young drug abuser, or, on the other hand, the lack of any right to comment on the ecstasy scene, since I come from a protected home and took only a few pills. I deny neither of these charges. My only defence is that this is the story of my eighteen-year-old mind, its vision and blindness. This is not a social history of the ecstasy trend, nor is it a 'my drug hell' sensation. It is what really happened – tall, white-haired Lennon offering to love me; a look of complicity from a beautiful, confident girl who made me feel I belonged; an initiation into a universe without boundaries.

I was born and raised in Oxford, both of my parents being dons at the university. My mother was a fellow of English and a biographer. My father was a professor of cellular pathology. I grew up to the sound of earnest talk over afternoon tea and 'formal halls'; no television except the news or the ballet on BBC2. And books. T. S. Eliot, Charlotte Brontë, Virginia Woolf, Chaucer and Jane Austen formed the reference points of our old-fashioned world. If I had a problem, my mother would quote poetry. I started writing stories, little books, magazines, poems and plays at the age of five, and had a drawer stuffed with books I had written by my seventh birthday. I knew I wanted to be a writer.

My parents, both descendents of Jewish immigrants from Lithuania to South Africa, had continued the Diaspora in the 1960s by migrating to New York and then to Oxford, where they had taken up their teaching posts. Every December we returned to Cape Town to be with my grandmother and extended family. My parents still loved South Africa, despite their haste to exit its apartheid. They still had some old, close friends in Cape Town.

Almost from birth I knew two young Capetonians, Cara Grey and Marc Miller. Cara's family was Jewish, like mine. Our grandmothers had been best friends throughout their lives, from the time they had been giggling gym-slipped schoolgirls at the Good Hope Seminary. Cara and I made up plays and formed secret clubs, and as we hit our teenage years, we exchanged long letters about boys: who we liked, who liked us. She would come to Passover or Shabbat at my gran's house. At fourteen, she was more sophisticated in manner and style than me, the difference between us being, it seemed to me, especially marked on these formal occasions. I was typically an embarrassment to myself, overweight and uncomfortable in a recherché Laura Ashley ensemble. Cara would be slim in a little black dress, her smooth black hair set off by her deep, lasting tan. At dinner I would be bouncy and bossy, muttering 'how disgusting to eat an ox's tongue' and demanding her romantic secrets. Cara would calmly tell me her naughty but innocent exploits. The most shocking was to kiss three boys one New Year's Eve. She was a good girl. She never seemed to have to try to find a 'get off'; rather boys pursued her and she, cautious and sage, refused them. Her world was ballet classes, days at the beach and suitors with names like Sean and Stefan. My world was a girls' school in Oxford, homework and academic expectations, silly pranks and, most of all, hoping to meet a boy who might prove 'deep'.

In fact, to my infinite sense of failure, my fourteen-year-old world was entirely boy-free. I never found a decent being among the sex-obsessed boys I kissed at parties. I did not have a single male friend other than my father – and Marc Miller. As a child Marc, the son of old friends of my parents, was slightly nerdy and chubby. We played Chinese chequers and I laughed at his farts. I liked his gentle, mellow company. At fifteen, he started an exercise programme and emerged as a sexy young man. He had shoulder-length blond hair and blue eyes, and loved grunge music. He resembled my idol, Kurt Cobain. In my all-hoping view, he was my future husband. Our parents tried to engineer a romance between us. We were allowed to sit undisturbed in Gran's garden on summer evenings, cloistered by heavily scented moonflowers and honeysuckle. The only problem was that he was shy with girls. On several occasions, I watched his arms wavering by his sides as we said goodbye after another chaste evening together discussing Nirvana, and willed them to rise into a hug, but he would only give me a little wave and promise to write.

Then on a routine family holiday when I was fifteen, life ignited. Suddenly that Easter I was thin and confident. Cara told me that she had met Marc: their two circles of friends had converged. Their nights were now filled with clubbing and dagga (the South African term for marijuana; pronounced dagha, with a guttural growl on the 'g').

Cara and her older, 'cool' school friend, Lizle, dressed me up in bell-bottoms and a hippie shirt and took me to The Playground, an 'industrial' club. We drank vodka and orange juice on balconies in Long Street, surrounded by fascinated 'guys'. The three of us strolled through Greenmarket Square in the sultry, incense-heavy heat during the days, while at night we smoked Peter Stuyvesants and then dagga in car parks behind the City Hospital. The drug had no effect on me. I was high on the thrill of going out in this glamorous, dangerous city. The first time I ever got stoned and felt it, the three of us were at the bungalow of Cara's friend Andre in the country town of Somerset West. There were fifteen of us sitting in his lounge passing around the joints. I was shy, being the youngest and most inexperienced person there. Andre and his cohorts made it their mission to get me 'trashed'. I smoked and drank and then suddenly had an enormous nose bleed. I was dashed. When the torrent was over, I relaxed and giggled uncontrollably, feeling my vision loosen. So this was being stoned. Cara became suspicious that Andre had spiked her drink and we were driven zigzaggingly back to Cape Town.

Cara was always ready to go out and have a 'kif' time, while still managing to keep to sensible rules. Unerringly polite, presentable and easy-going, she never drank or smoked too much, or compromised herself in any way. She never failed to enjoy herself and was the last to want to go home. While Cara was tall, slim and glamorous, with perfectly groomed long straight hair, Lizle was blonde and earthy. At the age of sixteen she had already grown up, been there and done that, and seemed almost maternal in her protectiveness and wisdom. She was the one who always knew whether we were safe or not. There was something husky and languid in her surf-girl manner. Above all, I loved it when she said 'hang ten'.

No-one I knew at home in Oxford smoked cannabis or wanted to go out anywhere other than our local 'Fifth Avenue', a chain of clubs that played Celine Dion remixes to boys in checked shirts and girls with perms and too much makeup. A few evenings after my night at Andre's, Marc, now seventeen, came for dinner at Gran's with his family. He was dressed in a heavy metal t-shirt and his blond hair was dishevelled. After dessert we retired to the 'nursery', my bedroom, and perched on the bed at a safe distance from each other. He impressed me with tales of druggie clubs where people openly shot up heroin. Marc loved Hendrix and The Doors. He said he had a friend called Lennon and the two of them were preparing to try LSD. They wanted to go through the doors of perception and had been studying Aldous Huxley for months. My crush grew. I was entranced. He was the only person of my acquaintance who seemed curious about life and committed to learning more. Marc asked if I wanted to meet up with him and Lennon the next day, my last before returning for the summer term in Oxford. I was overjoyed to be invited.

The following day I met the two grungy youths in a multi-story car park. Lennon was so tall that I could hardly see his face, but he was a striking figure with his natural blond afro. We smoked a spliff on the car park roof and then spent the afternoon wandering around the mall and sitting in a coffee shop, where I nibbled my way through half a bowl of brown sugar. While we were in a music shop we heard the news that Kurt Cobain had committed suicide. Outside again, it started to rain. I plaited my hair in pigtails and we ran through the streets. We ended up in the Cape Sun hotel bar, drinking vodka and orange. We talked about our searches for the meaning of life. We wanted to get lost in music. It was a world away from Oxford.

When I arrived home, I set up a Kurt Cobain shrine in my bedroom and wrote his initials in black felt tip ink on my wrist. Then I walked around the corner to the newsagent where my school friend Grace worked Sundays.

As I approached the till, I saw her head bowed over a celebrity magazine.

'You're back.' She barely looked up. Her long brown hair had been ruthlessly straightened with BaByliss tongs, and her eyes were red and itching from the shift from glasses to contacts. She had blown her nose through half a travel pack of tissues. There was a long pause. She seemed depressed.

I showed her my wrist, to make her laugh.

She found it hilarious that I was mourning him. 'I'm glad he's dead. Kurt Cobain was such a mad, gross freak.'

I knew better than to argue. I knew that beneath her suburban slump, she was relieved to have someone 'weird' in her life.

'So what's been happening here?'

'Same. Nothing. Terrible.' She turned the pages of her magazine.

'I really want to go to Glastonbury. D'you want to come with me?'

'Ugh. I can't think of anything worse. Think of all the crusties.'

'Please at least come to the Coven next weekend? It'll be so good.'

'Oh, I'll see.'

'We've got to change! There are other places to go than Park End, you know.'

'What for? Life is crapness.'

'But don't you want to . . . I mean why? How can you?'

'Not want to find my "inner self"?' mocked Grace in her clipped English accent.

'Look, I know it sounds stupid and naff and everything but if you'd just try . . . '

'Try *what*? Yoga? Meditation? Look, Olivia, I *like* shopping. I *like* Park End. I *like* falseness and posing and watching TV.' Sigh. 'Just fed up with everything. Welcome back, anyway. At least now I have someone to talk to again.'

She was so trapped in this closed-minded world she could

9

not see how life could be different. I realized how lucky I had been to see Cape Town.

The most I could convince my friends to do was a trip to Fifth Avenue – they all thought I was 'gay' for liking old music like the Doors. The boys at teenage parties were only interested in getting as far as possible. They professed to like Nirvana or Jimi Hendrix, so I thought they were nice and kissed them, but when they could not persuade me to have sex in a dark corner of the dance floor they dropped me without a backwards glance. Life was unbearably stagnant, and the only reality was writing long letters to Cara, Lizle and Marc and waiting for the next trip to Cape Town.

As I struggled with rat-like schoolboys and the manifest cruelties of those teenage parties, I would have been elated to know that Lennon had fallen in love with me. I did not discover this until the next time I saw him, the Christmas I was sixteen when we returned to South Africa. Sadly, one week before I arrived, he gave up waiting for me to write to him and started wooing a surly German tourist called Petra. I promptly fell in love with him, but it was too late.

That Christmas I knew what to expect. It was heady. Lennon and Marc were house-sitting in the bohemian suburb of Observatory ('Obs'). I stayed there with Lizle, Cara and another friend of the group, Elizabeth. Elizabeth was small, dark and intense. She made jewellery and was frequently depressed, while also wanting to have insane fun like all of us. We drank cocktails at 11 a.m. and partied all night. The house was overflowing with young bohemian adventurers, kittens and rainbow tie-dye. We were stoned all the time, smoking Swaziland grass from honeysuckle flowers and driving to the movies listening to Leonard Cohen. Endless flirting with gorgeous surfer types at indie clubs. The air was permanently scented with sandalwood incense. I sat on the garage roof with Lennon watching a fire on the mountain as 'Sweet Jane' played in the kitchen: 'Anyone who ever had a heart wouldn't turn around and break it.' He charmingly told me I was a goddess. He fell in love with Petra during those three weeks, but I was infatuated with him alone. He was so different from the boys back home, so original. He knew how to make me feel beautiful. His world was as intense as mine. He understood the pain of existence and he led the group in many joyful escapades.

On New Year's Eve we went to a rave. The boys took their first acid trip, while I shared a wrap of speed with Elizabeth. It helped me stay up all night. In the morning, I found myself cleaning the kitchen singing Oasis's 'Supersonic'. When Lennon entered the room, I felt a crackle of electricity. He stumbled in, utterly dishevelled yet charged with preternatural energy. Marc followed him like a piece of cement jittering in the wake of a bomb. Lennon strode to the fridge and exploded the top off a can of lager. He gulped it down without a pause. Marc giggled and stretched. Lennon leaned against the kitchen table sybaritically, surveying the neatness of the room.

'Hi . . . ' he said at last. 'Shit . . . this is . . . intense . . . I can't . . . '

Marc cracked up at some secret joke.

'When did you take it?' I asked.

'Uhhh . . . a long, long, long time ago . . . ja . . . ' nodded Marc, making a real effort to appear lucid.

'Ja, he means five hours ago,' interrupted Lennon, beaming.

Lennon and Marc annoyed me, telling me I was plastic.

11

. They refused to stop rambling about the multicoloured fish on the ceiling. Suddenly I looked in the mirror and saw my face was covered in red dots. I felt feverish. I got a taxi back to Gran's, where I was promptly diagnosed with chicken pox.

Each time my family returned to Cape Town after that, it was similar but never quite as bewitching. I remained madly and constantly in love with Lennon but he was only sometimes interested in me, and never wrote to me when I left. He was a charismatic and popular boy who had an energy, a drive and idealism that only he possessed. He was poetic and played guitar. In his band, Hectic Peace, he sang the songs he had written in a style of his own, half Elvis Presley and half Jim Morrison, in his mellifluous voice. His look, entirely uncultivated, was so unusual that passers-by often turned to stare at him. He was six feet, four inches tall, with a pale, painfully thin body and, most attention-grabbing of all, he had a blond afro the size of a 1970s paper light shade. He refused to cut his hair for anyone. It was not a matter of vanity, since the hair won him far more derision than praise. In fact the uncut, seriously out-of-control hair was an emblem of his resistance to societal oppression. He cared nothing for outward appearances, including his own. His life was romantic and dedicated to escaping 'the system', and he was depressed most of the time because it was impossible. The tyrannical voices of rule-makers and the media crush the spirit, he told me. I had never encountered anything so radical outside poetry. His philosophy was mysterious, terrifying. It seemed to open my eyes to something immense.

'Can you handle knowing?' he would scoffingly ask, sitting

at the kitchen table in his house-sit as we brooded to Pink Floyd's 'The Wall'.

He knew me better than I knew myself. He knew I was a double-edged girl, told me I was bohemian in spirit but voluptuous in sense. He derided my love of comfort, my dependence on an abundant flow of cash and my un-hermit-like attitude. In the custom of men, he always cast me as an Eve, tempting him away from his deep principles towards the pleasures of the flesh. It was thrilling.

One day back in lonely, peaceful Oxford, when I was sixteen, my father asked me what my friends and I talked about.

'We talk about a secret,' I said, 'something normal adults don't ever think about. You wouldn't understand. There's this whole universe of mystery. I never heard of it until I met Lennon and read T. S. Eliot.'

I was thinking of the phrases from *The Waste Land* with which I had grown up in academic Oxford – shantih shantih shantih, the peace that passeth understanding, and the key turning once in each man's prison.

My father was flabbergasted at my naiveté.

'Come on Olivia,' he laughed incredulously. 'Are you telling me you think no-one else in the world apart from Lennon and T. S. Eliot ever considered the meaning of life? Your mom and I, when we were exactly your age, well we would stay up all night with our friends just threshing it all out. It's what all teenagers do.'

I was embarrassed, but fought back: 'There, you see, it's just "what teenagers do". I am never going to get to twenty-five and be a bland, normal person who has closed their mind. I promise. And Lennon won't either.'

My father only laughed kindly.

With each trip to Cape Town, the drug scene became bigger. Nothing was going to stop us in our search for life's mysteries so taboo to 'the system', and in our circle, drugs were the magic key to those doors of perception. We thought taking drugs was cool – the more the better. A year after my first spliff, I had my first taste of acid. I was sixteen. By this time, Lennon and Marc were taking it every weekend in the forest. I wanted admittance to their secret.

The night arrived cool and cloudless. Refreshed and wearing a combination of Cara, Lizle and Elizabeth's clothes, I sat in Marc's car. Marc was at the wheel, so the car was veering merrily, music pounding, windows wide open, as we spiralled lower and lower down Table Mountain. Far below, the Atlantic reflected the city lights. As the car speeded up to a frenetic 150 kilometres per hour, Marc seemed to lose control.

'Shitshitshitshitshit,' he muttered.

'That's it, I'll drive,' ordered Lennon. 'Stop the car.'

Obediently, Marc screeched the car to a halt and swapped seats with Lennon. Unfortunately, Lennon's driving was even worse.

As the car swerved along, Marc reached into the glove compartment and pulled out a miniscule tinfoil package. He lovingly unwrapped it to reveal two paper squares, each printed with a picture of a red strawberry with a green stalk. Brandishing a stolen pair of his mother's nail scissors, he proceeded to cut each strawberry into three segments. The biggest one was automatically fed to Lennon, I noticed. Then he took his third. The next one went to Elizabeth and the one after that to

Lizle. Finally he handed me a piece. I was pleased to see that it contained a pretty pink section of the strawberry. Taking a deep breath and trying to block out the parental warnings going through my mind, I placed it on my tongue. It did not taste of anything. Somehow I had expected a fiery sizzle and immediate hallucinations, but nothing happened. 'I've done it,' I thought. 'It's too late now.'

We arrived at our destination, a rave, having stopped along the way to buy four lollipops each. The queue outside looked at least a quarter of a mile long. Thousands of people talked over the distant pound of the music. Almost all the men had shaved heads, bare chests and super-baggy trousers. The women looked like futuristic dolls in their glitter makeup and gold, silver or plastic dresses. In their pigtailed hair they wore children's hairclips. Surreptitiously Lizle, Elizabeth and I adjusted our own. A stream of ravers flowed out from inside, sodden with foam and sweat, nodding their heads manically, marching down the queue in rhythm with the music. Voices floated over me . . .

'It's lank packed in there, man.'

'Fuckin' amazin'!'

'Rushin' off her face, she is.'

An English voice: 'All right mate, they're really 'avin' it in there.'

It had been three-quarters of an hour since we had taken the trip. I had timed it to the minute. I wasn't feeling anything yet, but how could I be sure?

Lennon and Marc seemed separate, as if they were on a different plane of reality altogether. They were talking closely behind us girls in the queue.

'It's too *hectic*,' Lennon was saying. 'Shall we go to the mountain after all?'

'Ja. Kom,' Marc agreed.

They started to walk away without saying goodbye.

'Lennon?' I called after him. He half turned to meet my eyes.

'We're going to the mountain, Olivia,' he said, looking straight at me with an intensity I found unsettling. 'We'll pick you up at 6 a.m. in the car park.'

They left. Look at the stars, I told myself. The sky was so clear, not hazy at all, just deep black. The stars were burning silver. The mountain was so red I almost could not look at it, and in the tiny layer of clouds behind it were pictures of people: a mother and baby, a man gardening, a woman dancing. They were not hallucinations – I knew they were only clouds – but they had some indefinable subtlety I had never noticed before.

It was all clear. People were sharp and defined, the voices around me piercing. It all rushed at me so quickly I could not keep track.

'This is it,' I thought. 'I'm tripping. And I've never felt so good in my life.'

My seven acid trips were almost all good. I usually took half a gold microdot or strawberry, once a whole microdot in two doses twelve hours apart. Lennon and Marc were taking up to two trips at a time every Saturday. Some of my trips I took in the forest, others in house clubs and raves amid teenagers decorated with luminous body paint, rubbing one another with deep heat gel and inhaling the heavy scent of amyl nitrate. I never took more than half a dot at a time because I was partly aware of the dangers. Yet I felt invincible. I loved the risk. The frequent presence of Lennon and Marc, with their acceptance of whatever might come, made it feel safe. There were no real hallucinations for me; rather, I experienced journeys through the different stages of the trip, from laughter to dancing to philosophizing, and a sensation of sharpened reality like putting on a pair of glasses. It was as if it made no difference to me, as if I were already naturally tripping. Yet I did see a few fractals when I closed my eyes. I had one worrying hour when a boy in a club walked off after kissing me and never came back. I froze, unable to respond to anyone. I felt my world disintegrate. It was a 'freak-out'. Luckily Lizle's boyfriend, Warren, was an experienced acid taker and knew what to do. He talked me through it. Soon I was feeling better than I had originally, for having broken through the problem. Freak-outs were an accepted part of our trips. Our group felt no need to pretend to be happy or to be anything we were not. These was the kind of friendships I had always wanted.

Once at 4.30 in the morning at a chill-out club called Gel, while everyone lay comatose staring at fractals projected on the wall, we saw a woman in her mid-twenties dancing with unusual vigour, almost as if she were showing off her lack of inhibition. Lizle glanced at me knowingly. 'Just look at that. She is definitely e-ing,' she whispered to me. A week later we went to a rave. I came across Lizle and her friend Ellen in a field, breathlessly turning cartwheels in the lasers. Neither seemed to recognize me. They were giggling hysterically, chasing the laser light, impatiently motioning for me to get out of their way. I laughed. 'Lizle – what are you on!?' My friend merely bounced up and down on the spot, stretching to the sky, burbling, 'Oh my god! Oh my god! Oh my god!' She seemed a different person. I walked away eventually, tired of being ignored. An hour later, I saw her again and she gazed at me in wonder like a child looking up into a sky of snowflakes. 'You look like a fairy,' she cried. It was the first time I saw one of my friends on ecstasy.

Back at my girls' school in Oxford, I reached out to everyone I could, but people found me too intense. My friends liked shoe-shopping and pop music, while I didn't know how to be girly. My school was one of the top five for exam results in the country. It was nothing more than an academic factory farm: education was spoon-fed to us. Our classes were not always interesting; they did not need to be. The reason for the school's success was its selection of hard-working, ambitious pupils from donnish backgrounds who would never dare to fail. We were discouraged from studying drama, art or music, and science stood above the arts. English was my favourite subject. After several years with teachers who plodded line by line through *Moonfleet* or *The Admirable Crichton*, and whose marking style was to write nothing but 'B+ Good' at the end of an essay, I was pleased when Miss McArthur joined the staff. She asked us to find a short-story writer we admired and report on why we had made that choice. She set us Wilfred Owen and Thomas Hardy, and classes were suddenly alive with discussion instead of morose voices droning aloud mediocre books about smugglers.

'Sort it out Olivia, you'll never beat the system,' my classmate Debbie would call out to me on a daily basis, guffawing at my crowd-pleasing tales of drugs and madness. Five years before, in our first year, she had called me 'grease pot' and 'frecks', homing in on my oily hair and freckled face. There were three rigidly distinct groups in my year at school. The 'Heavy Gang', of which Debbie was a stalwart, were the girls who grew up early. They had boyfriends at twelve, wore make-up to school and had no ambitions. They were the kind of girls who called you 'gross' if you had a torn pair of tights. By the time they left school, this group was already beginning to look faded and suburban. They uniformly followed one of two routes, either business or the dole.

Then there was the 'Cumnor Lot'. This was the 'geeky' group of shy, mousy girls and misfits, many of whom lived on the outskirts of Oxford, in the hilltop village of Cumnor. These girls were sweet, but they never dared to break a school rule or go out with boys. After leaving school, they broke out and pursued successful careers at Oxbridge, in the City or as classical musicians.

I was a member of neither group. I was too short, gauche and bookish to join the Heavy Gang, and too rebellious for the Cumnor Lot. I remained among the ten or so other girls who were neither cool nor geeks. Our group had no name, since we changed it continually. There was Grace, super-organized, clever, whom everyone predicted would become a high-flying executive. Leila, a lively, laughing girl who could make a joke of anything and was effortlessly trendy. She later crossed over into the Heavy Gang. Mitsuko, the beautiful Japanese girl who got 100 per cent in exams and had a charming, wicked nature. Maggster was a plump girl who wore jumpsuits and liked to go ice skating. Then there was Kay, who was wonderfully normal, like a girl next door, and Arianne, who was scarily sarcastic.

In our group, which lasted from age eleven to the sixth

form, we shared sleepovers, fights and eating disorders. We worked hard at our studies, experimented with mass masturbation while listening to Madonna's 'Erotic', and went to our first teenage parties together. The bitching within our group and between all three groups was savage. It was quite normal to arrive at school one morning and find no-one was speaking to you and notes were circulating against you. Several days later you would discover it was because you wore the wrong kind of bra, or because everyone had decided you were a lesbian (to be called gay was meant to be the worst insult of all). I used to tell my mother she wouldn't last a day at school. There was no pastoral care. The school cared only about our academic results.

As we grew older, the pressure narrowed to our appearance. The rule came from the media, Sweet Valley High books featuring 'perfect size six' blonde teens, and, worst of all, it came from one another. You had to wear the 'cool' clothes, be the accepted weight (eight stone or under), have glossy hair and the right accessories. One day we were scruffy, childlike twelve-year-olds, running on adventures through the school, making magazines and exploding with laughter. The next day we started passing 'slam books', anonymously noting down which of our classmates were 'prettiest' or 'ugliest', 'most likely to meet a hunky seventeen-year-old' or 'most resembling a scrambled egg'. The day after that, we all looked in the mirror and saw for the first time how the world saw us. A piece of young woman, to be cruelly assessed, lower than another girl because you wore glasses and she was seven stone. That was the day our mass, secret diet of insecurity started, as we bowed in submission to the rule of society. Our group bursts of creativity dampened and our laughter turned snide as each girl retreated into her private adolescence. By the age of fifteen, most of us had turned ourselves out respectably. Losing weight and learning to use makeup had become our art.

The distant family world I knew in South Africa had always been more glittery than Oxford, peopled by smooth, bejewelled white madams I would overhear ordering another drink from their servants as they lazed by the pool. At one party hosted by wealthy stockbrokers a few years earlier, I had been introduced to a group of boys who had been sent to school in England. I asked one what he thought of London.

'It's a bit *noir*,' he smirked.

Those scenes had the glassy, horrible intrigue for me of a bluebottle jellyfish, the kind that floated in the Indian Ocean or studded the beaches dead in droves, a synthetic shade of blue with stinging ribbon tentacles.

In Jewish South Africa, everyone looked great. On dusky Shabbat evenings, the scent of Amarige mingled with the honeysuckle around Gran's spiral garden staircase up to her 'Sun Room', as slender teenagers selected Black Magic chocolates. Gran would eat her chocolate by slicing it into slivers on a plate, savouring each miniscule smudge. 'I weighed seventy-five pounds at your age,' she once told me disapprovingly when I was twelve, on hearing my weight was in excess of one hundred pounds. As I grew up, I primped and preened to match my relatives' glamour. Lennon was the first teenage male I found, either in Oxford or Cape Town, who did not judge people on appearance. He found some women beautiful and others not, but he was not like the boys I had always met, who thought women were two-dimensional magazine models. He was a comforting, inspiring idol.

I moved from my private girls' school to a good local comprehensive halfway through my penultimate year of school, partly in a search for people who would be like my South African friends. The teaching was better, since the teachers could not rely on their pupils' diligence, but had to stimulate their interest. I did meet a few nice people, but it was hard to come in mid-year in the sixth form when cliques were already in place. A few classmates resented me for coming from a private school, and it could not be denied I was a middle-class Jewish girl, although I was, in my heart, as far from being a snob as possible. My naïve philosophy was one of adventure with no concern for material things. In this I was following Lennon, whose life purpose was to 'escape the system'. Yet my English classmates, for the most part, assumed I was a prim posh girl. South Africans had never judged me in this way, not being party to the British class system in which a person with the wrong accent or who went to the wrong school is instantly made to feel an alien.

Somehow, every time I went out with my new classmates, I made a fool of myself, probably because of the pressure to be 'cool'. I would cough on my cigarette or throw up after drinking: in South Africa these things would not have drawn the slightest censure from my friends, only further friendliness, but the next day at school there would be turned backs and cold faces. There was a girl named Tanya who had been new the year before but by going out with a popular boy had entered the elite of the cool group. I had thought her quite nice and was pleased when she invited me on a night out with the girls in Oxford city centre. I drank a few alcopops with the group and then Tanya took me to visit her boyfriend, Bill, who lived around the corner from me. Down in his basement bedroom, he and a friend were smoking spliffs. I happily partook, and then half an hour later, when the friend left, Bill and Tanya said they would walk me home. Halfway down his street, I had a white-out. I suddenly could walk no further, felt sick and completely devoid of energy. It had never happened to me before but I later learnt it sometimes happens to cannabis smokers who have been drinking. Appearing kind and concerned, Tanya and Bill led me the short distance home and up to my room.

The weekend passed and on Monday I returned to school. I saw Tanya in the playground and went up to her.

'How are you?' I started.

She glanced at me with her eyebrow raised. 'Yeah, fine. You feeling better? You really scared us on Friday.'

'Oh yes,' I said, 'I was fine in the end.'

'OK then. See ya.'

Courtesy over, she spun on her heel and stalked away. She never approached me again. Every time I tried to talk to her, her boyfriend or one of her friends, they signalled a cold 'you're sad'. My inability to hold my smoke that night was obviously my downfall.

I remained close to my old girls' school friends and we sometimes went out to The Coven, one of the only dance music clubs in Oxford. We would take strong speed and dance for hours on the podium in our micro miniskirts and platforms. Speed had no psychological effect on me, only the physical effect of making it effortless to dance for four or five hours non-stop. We would start out at a naff bar like The Set. A gram of speed would be swallowed, mixed into a cocktail glass of water. We would then walk briskly to The Coven where we waited apathetically on the balcony overlooking the dance floor, impatient for the drug's onset. It would manifest itself suddenly with a dramatic lightening of the weight of the fingers and feet. Buoyant, our limbs would become elastic, electric, itching to dance. Not wanting to waste a second, we would rush down onto the platform dance floor and let the speed work its cool magic. Sweat would be pouring down my back and I would discover blisters on my feet the next day, but at the time I was like an indomitable ice-cube. The come-downs were unpleasant and we were jittery on Sundays. Yet they never lasted or became unbearable.

I took ecstasy about three times the year I was sixteen but each one was either a dud or I never 'came on'. They had no effect. It was the peak of adolescence for me. My main worries were that no-one was in love with me, that I was hideous and that I didn't have enough friends. I went out with my first two boyfriends only because they liked me, even though I felt nothing for them. I knew drugs were dangerous, but thought being self-destructive was cool. My parents worried about me. They did not know I was taking drugs but they disapproved of my 'prostitute' going-out clothes, smoking and late nights. My mother found I had sneaked out one night to meet a boy. They sent me to see a counsellor but I stopped going and pocketed the money they gave me for her. They grounded me and I ran away to Glastonbury with some crusties who lived behind Oxford railway station.

I managed to climb over a fence to get into the festival and met some people from school. All I had taken with me was my bag with some shampoo and my comb in it so I could have a shower. When I returned to the crusties in the car park to collect the rest of my things, the van had disappeared. I spent the day searching for them from one end of the valley to the other. Eventually I called my sister, who was beyond fury. She told me my mother had the police looking for me. I hitchhiked to Yeovil to catch a train home, oblivious to what I was doing to my family. When my mother met me at the station she was silent with disappointment. I apologized, but I had pushed my family and friends to their limits, and it was hard to regain their approval.

On reading this account almost ten years later, my mother wrote to me: 'This seems to me wrong – the police phoned and said they were putting you on a train because the crusties had stolen your money. They gave you or you bought some coloured pencils to while away the time en route. I remember that meeting at the station, as you came down the stairs from platform two, you gave me a half-worried, half off-hand semi-smile. I was so thankful to see you safe that disapproval paled. The long-term effect was that I feared your running away again. This may have led to what I believe you call spoiling. In fact I did have a definite policy with you. I decided that it was best to support you – even if it felt to me a bit excessive. I believe that policy worked up to a point in that you knew you could trust us to love and care for you. I saw that opposition might blunt or damage your teenage mechanism – my decision was to go "with" you. But the danger of course was your lack of protection.'

I was grateful for my family's loving treatment of me

through this time, but nothing could hide the distress I was causing them. The more liberal and kind they were, the more exploitative, ashamed and self-hating I became. I was yearning for idealistic principles and explored these by writing poetry, plays and stories, as I always had. This was the only constructive element of my life. People borrowed money from me and never returned it. Boys picked me up and dropped me, although I was wise enough not to sleep with them. By the time of my seventeenth birthday I was mentally hibernating until I could leave school and live in Cape Town.

Finally, I flew out there the day of my last A-level exam and stayed with Gran. I was seventeen and a half and it was the first time I had left my parents for so long. The first week was difficult, adjusting to a new set of people. Lennon was going out with another girl, but I convinced myself I was over him. Then the Grahamstown Festival appeared on the horizon.

Chapter Two

For two weeks every July, the small university town of Grahamstown, halfway along the coast between Cape Town and
Durban, becomes South Africa's leading arts playground. To
the intelligentsia it is a cultural *hajj*, while to the young, it is
a fortnight-long party. Cara and her friend Mandy had
secured jobs selling jewellery at the main market in a large
field. I wandered around all day reading 'Zen' tarot for
donations. All my friends were there and Lennon was on the
point of breaking up with his girlfriend. I was in love with
him, but denied this to myself as well as to him and his girl,
since the one thing he valued above all was independence.
He followed a creed I always saw pinned up in Cape Town
hippy homes about how 'Love is letting go . . . you go your
way and I'll go mine, and if by some chance we find each
other, that's wonderful'. I thought this was rubbish: love was
passionate and would bind itself to its object. Yet if I could
just pretend I had no interest in him, he might fall back in
love with me.

Mandy . . . Mandy was a revelation. People who take ecstasy
say that everyone almost falls in love with their mentor, the
first person who introduces them to the drug. Mandy was that

person who won my admiration and gratitude. To me, Mandy was ecstasy. The first time I met her was the night I arrived in Cape Town. Cara took me to a rave in the Three Arts theatre in the suburb of Plumstead. It was to be a low-key night; no drugs. I did not take drugs when I was out with Cara because she was too wary of their dangers to take anything. She was a party person without needing them. Before the rave she took me to a pre-party at a boy's flat. It was the first time I met Cape Town's e-people at close quarters.

As we walked into the living room I saw a turntable playing incredibly clean-sounding house. The beats were perfect: sharp and discrete. The TV had cartoons showing with the sound muted. About twenty e-kids were sitting up in nice armchairs and a boy who seemed to personify the whole scene was moving almost professionally from person to person, shaking their hands and welcoming them to the party. It was clinically polite. You could not fault it – these people believed in manners and love and good things. The room was full of élan. But it was also intimidating and lacked any genuine warmth. They were all so flawlessly good looking, these boys with their baggy combat trousers and bare or meshed vest-covered, tanned and honed chests. The girls looked like Barbie dolls with lollipops and plastic hairgrips. They, too, were frighteningly poised and toned. Not one bit like the British kids you'd see on a Saturday night back home. There was not a black face among them, but this was usual in this elite circle of a victorious race, although they were in no way racist since they all believed in equality, freedom and the New South Africa. One of the girls was Mandy. Tall, white, slender, languid, tanned: a privileged Stellenbosch girl. She had bobbed mousey hair that looked wild yet utilitarian. She drawled in a drugged-out voice, 'Wooooww. Raaaaaaaaad.' *Rad* was her word and later mine. She pronounced the word with such range of pitch and melody and utter expressiveness it sounded like she was having an orgasm. Her eyes would scrunch together and then open in wonder as she spoke it, like a child.

When I next saw her in Grahamstown, we were living with eight other people in a two-room cottage. Marc and Lennon's girlfriend were sleeping in Marc's car, parked wherever they chose. It made me laugh to tap on the windscreen in the mornings and watch them shoot the car seats up into upright. Lennon was camping in his own tent, ever the hermit. Mandy was hooked on ecstasy. Not in any addicted way, but it had her in an emotional hug. She told me all about it. How you sucked the pill in your mouth until it dissolved. You came on and felt a rush. This was not like any rush I might have experienced on speed or acid. 'Ja, this is a RUSH!' she said in her cool, blissed-out voice as if she were feeling it then and there. 'Mmmmmm . . . ' I wanted to know if there were any dangers. I knew of the death of Leah Betts, apparently from drinking too much water while on ecstasy, as well as tales of other ecstasy casualties, but I wanted to hear a raver's point of view. 'Nothing bad's ever happened to me,' she said, 'but you might feel like you need to be hospitalized when you rush. But that soon passes and it's just a feeling. Just drink a little water – not too much – and you'll have a rad time, ok?' She gave me that cheeky complicit look as if I was going to be let into the biggest secret in the universe.

So one night her contact gave us an extra vanilla cream and I took a sixth. Marc, a girl called Janine and I drove to the Power

Station. This was a warehouse rave-club set in a green area. It blurred in my memory into no more than that, and even at the time, I was barely observant of what constituted the outside space. Upstairs was a dance floor and chill-out annexe and downstairs my only memory is more dancing and people mingling. In we went and onto the dance floor. I wasn't feeling anything. So we all trooped back to the car to smoke a spliff in a different surrounding. As we smoked, that's when it happened: one of the best moments of my life.

First a stray thought crossed my mind: 'I love this car.' I was thinking of how Marc's Golf had driven us to so many good times. Then I heard the music from the club. It was a trance melody that was to haunt me for weeks as I struggled to remember it but never quite could. It simply sounded like the most wonderful thing I had ever heard. I was overcome by an unspeakably massive wave of passion that still sends a shiver down my spine. I was living the existence I had always wanted. All those years of dreaming of breaking free, somehow, being myself, somehow, were over. I was authentic at last. Everything was now. My body could do whatever it wanted. No inhibitions. None of that mattered anymore. All that mattered was this feeling. A sense of effervescent excitement showered down beautifully into me like a snowstorm. Within a split second I was following this instinct, tumbling out of the car joyfully crying, 'Oh my god! The music! I've got to go to the music!' My friends giggled, understanding what was happening. 'Here we go! Olivia's first e,' said Janine.

Rejoicing with them, I ran almost desperately across the green towards the music. I was stumbling and almost falling, but physical constraints were as nothing to me and I did not care how I looked. It was a beatific moment of identity. Unprompted, like a mantra, the words 'it's me' repeated in my head as I ran. Within those moments I had a flashback to infancy of which I was barely aware at the time, but which came back to me in the following months as if I had opened a door to memory. I was an innocent child again, free of all fear. The song 'Wuthering Heights' by Kate Bush was playing in this memory. 'It's me . . . I've come home.' It was no specific time, but rather a sense of childhood flashing before my eyes, and this was the symbolic theme song. It was the world of the late 1970s. Leg-warmers and leotards. Running free in the cosy house in November and so many new things everywhere. All things were fresh and immeasurably beautiful. It was a bell ringing, calling me back to a time before shame. I only identified the song weeks later: it was not a song I listened to, but doubtless my sister, thirteen when I was born, had enjoyed it when it was popular in 1978 – the year I was born. After taking ecstasy it became 'my' song. I bought the album for my eighteenth birthday and listened to it nostalgically, recalling emotive memories. This flashback happened in the space of a second or two as I was running.

Then I was at the entrance to the club and saw some acquaintances. I was still stunned by my feelings, and kept thinking, 'This is ecstasy. Ecstasy is ecstasy, in the truest sense of the word.' Here assiduous memory, grafted by what was to come in the months that followed, fails. They were all surrounded by rainbows like haloes. I later questioned whether or not those people I did not trust in 'real life' also had rainbows transfiguring them. This was something that later bothered me: did I see false beauty? Why did I see false beauty? Who had

31

I even seen? I could not and can not remember. I greeted them ecstatically and glided upstairs to the music. I was aware of having a rapt expression on my face. As I went up a young man passed me on his way down. His rapt expression was a mirror. We shared a wordless moment of revelation in which we each understood the other was rushing, and gazed at each other in wonder.

Upstairs I could not co-ordinate my body to dance other than a muted forward and back and side-to-side step. My mind was too busy to think of more imaginative ways of dancing – it had no space. It was full.

I went into the chill-out room and played with a girl's hair. I was starting to feel calmer and more normal, although still absolutely schmangled, as we used to put it. Meandering back outside, I looked for Lennon. I found myself wandering lost and quite alone in the dark field, walking and then crawling along some concrete structures or tree stumps. My body was so out of control it seemed it might topple. Lennon came into view, sitting in a van with one of the market-sellers, a gun-loving man who had struck me before as creepy. The salesman made some salacious remark about my out-of-it state and I felt – what? Again this moment, looking back, made me wonder. Did I realize he was unpleasant, or did I just think 'never mind, I love everyone' and so compromise honesty? I no longer remember but this question tormented me months later when I became depressed. The first moments until I reached the club were perfect but the tarnishing of that night began within five minutes of coming on and gradually increased over the six months that followed until I was in the grip of a breakdown.

Lennon was being unfriendly and I asked why. He answered that I was not being myself. At this stage he was anti-ecstasy. He found the rave-bunnies superficial and thought me one of them. To him ecstasy was a drug of conformism, of the system – not that he had ever taken it, but judging from the dolled-up people who did. Six months later, I would be the one to criticize the drug while he would look more kindly upon its effects. That night I wandered off again and finally, near dawn, returned to my room. By this time Cara, Mandy and I were renting a stationary railway carriage in a party train, since we had been thrown out of the cottage for our irresponsible antics. As I fell asleep I strained to hear that song again but it was to elude me forever. The song made a picture in my mind of a delicate flower's petals opening and I tried to play this image to hear the music again but that heavenly melody was gone, though I still sensed its echoes.

The next day I woke up without any kind of hangover – in fact I was still soaring. Insecurity felt a thing of the past. My life until the night before was like a small grey town over which a colossal snowball had rolled. In the wake of this avalanche was this first day of the future. When I looked back all I could see was a monumental ball of snow obliterating the past. My teenage years seemed over. I was reborn.

That day I practically skipped from the train into town. Money and gifts were flowing from my hand into those of street-children as never before. I sat around doodling hearts and 'I love E' all over any paper I could find. In the evening I smoked a spliff with everyone and a last vestige of the 'loved-up' sensation fluttered through me like a butterfly. I 'went off' again, soaring gently. What a drug! To have a comedown that was almost as good as the high was a miracle.

A few days later, amid more ecstasy and acid trips, Lennon broke up with his girlfriend. He told me he was once more in love with me. We all returned to Cape Town after the Grahamstown Festival. Lennon and I started going out. I made new friends of all races, including two impoverished young sisters, Anne and Jen (we called them Ann 'n' Jen). They were only fifteen and thirteen, but were so precocious that they appeared and behaved like women of twenty. Their mother Christiane was a Swiss psychologist turned flower farmer; their father a Xhosa farm labourer who had deserted the family. Christiane remarried and worked hard to care for the girls and their younger stepsisters, but money was scarce and their new stepfather was a hateful man. He sometimes threw Ann 'n' Jen off the farm, leaving them roaming Cape Town's insalubrious streets late at night with nowhere to go unless they trusted a stranger. They grew up too young, never staying in school long enough to pass exams, smoking grass, hitchhiking, and hanging around clubs and festivals with their urban family.

No child could have asked for a mightier home than the flower farm, which contained mountains, waterfalls, butterflies and baboons. Invited for a weekend, I saw for the first time the blue-black depth of a night sky shielded by mountains from towns' artificial light. Every star of the southern constellations blazed across it. Yet in the dusty farmhouse, Ann 'n' Jen and their little, wide-eyed, half-wild stepsisters slept in one makeshift pile of mattresses and old blankets. There was no hot water, no fridge, and only a gas camping stove for cooking.

Meals were freshly harvested vegetables and rice. The girls left weekly for boarding school in Wolseley at five on a Monday morning: quite the opposite of a smart school, it was a harsh one for poor farmers' children. The five of them crouched in the back of an open 'bakkie' truck as it rattled for an hour over rough farm roads before reaching the world outside, dawn slowly lighting the valley yellow-green.

They were the wildest girls I had ever met. Anne was fun, calm and strong-minded. She looked like a Native American and possessed a wisdom beyond her years. Jen was younger and more volatile. At thirteen, she was flirtatious and confident, and would entertain our group of eighteen-year-olds with her patter. '*Oops*, I *dropped* my *pencil*,' she would suggestively over-stress, raising her eyebrows as she let her pencil fall to the floor. A born actress, she had a gift for imitating the voices of the New South Africa. My favourite of her characters was 'Shannon', the Kugel (the South African equivalent of a Jewish American Princess). 'Shannon' would begin in a high-pitched tone: 'I like tomato-red shoes. Do you know aye was sitting at Meriel's hairdressers' the other day and do you know what aye heard about *Jackie*? She's running off with a *black*. Now I know, I know that it's the New South Efrica and all thet, and we can let the blacks work in our gardens now, and not be careful they might steal our roses and give them to their girlfriends, but you can't *sleep* with the man for heaven's sake and have an affair on your *white lawyer* husband who's giving you the best fucking years – excuse my language, praise the lord, but the best fucking years in your whole *entire* life. You know, she wants to go with the raggle-taggle-gypsies-*oh*. Now there are only two things that aye hite about Seth

Africa – and that's apartheid – and the blacks.' The room of African, Afrikaner and Jewish teenagers would erupt in hysterical laughter.

A hardcore hippie couple in their forties, Rod and Juliette, invited Lennon and I to their home for dinner twice. Lennon had met them in Grahamstown, where they had served him lentil curry and *rotis* in their tent. The nooks and crannies of their bungalow's kitchen were piled with folded plastic wrappings, papers and compost for recycling. The walls were decorated with paintings by the couple. A scent of incense and wet dog wafted through the room as we were served rice covered with a vast mound of plain boiled spinach. At the same time, in one of the corners, their dog was fed pungent meat that smelt rotten. They considered seasoning an insult to the wholesomeness of the vegetables, and insisted that we eat using chopsticks. I asked if I could please, please use a knife and fork, having no proficiency with the chopsticks and noting, to my embarassment, that the pile of spinach on my plate was barely diminishing. That was Rod and Juliette's chance to tell me exactly why eating with chopsticks was the rule around here.

'It makes you eat more slowly so you can digest your meal properly,' Juliette said. 'You can't use cutlery. It is time you learnt.'

So I resumed eating the limp spinach strand by strand. Still the mound would not diminish and yet everyone else's plate was clear.

'Don't you like your veggies?' teased Rod. 'I suppose you're used to all that processed rubbish.'

'No, no, it's delicious,' I protested faintly, my voice coming out far too stiff. Under the table Lennon squeezed my hand.

Where I came from, vegan cuisine might involve a Thai stir-fry or veggie-burgers. In this world, your commitment to the cause was tested by your ability to down harvest quantities of unsalted boiled greens.

After supper I offered to wash up. It seemed expected of me in this communist household. After I had cleaned up, we closed all doors and windows and smoked, creating a hotbox. Rod put on some 'world music'. We danced and talked about the ideal of peace and love. I started to relax.

It was the first of many similar encounters with hardcore hippies I was to have in the years that followed.

After years at home, I was now 6,000 miles away, free and independent and seventeen and a half. Almost grown up, but I lived with Gran. She was sweet and tragic, having lost much of her memory. My heart would ache to find her wandering in her room, asking for a friend who had died. Sometimes she would remember and would cry in my arms, saying, 'All my friends are dead.' She was fed, bathed and given her medicines by a series of uninspired carers who seemed to understand very little. We only kept her social life going by continuing to hold the weekly Shabbat dinner for which she had been renowned for half a century. Cara, Lennon and Marc would be invited, and always my cousins. As the meals progressed, Gran would unwittingly provoke my mother's cousin Bobby to insane annoyance by repeatedly asking, to her minute-by-minute timetable, if he would like another helping. We young people laughed and cried with her, sensing her as one of us, a drifter on a cosmic ocean of life and death.

31 July 1996

Dear Grace,

Thanks for your letter & card I got today & for the Pro-plus (much needed!), photos etc. The first thing I did with the Pro-plus was to take it over to a drug addict's house (Lennon's), put 10 pills in a saucer, take a pestle and grind them into a fine white powder. We then rolled up a crisp R50 banknote (we thought a R100 note would have been more appropriate – yuppies & all that – but the only one available was too crumpled) and snorted the Pro-plus in lines. It didn't do much & burnt my nose, so I'm now taking them normally.

It was strange looking at the photos – a lot of people look like strangers, it seems everyone has changed so much, or maybe in reality they just don't correspond with the images of them I have in my mind.

Things are fine here. The job situation has gone haywire. (This is not actually fine at all . . .)

Loads has happened. To put it briefly, I'm going out with Lennon (we got together on Saturday 27th). It's perfect & we're completely in love with each other . . . dreamy.

I've got to sleep now – going clubbing much later & need a rest.

Lots of love,

Olivia xxx

Cape Town was where the cool kids came to party. Where else were clubbers so polished? I had always feared being disliked. The clubbers' creed was acceptance and 'being yourself', but until I tried ecstasy, I found this fake, coming as it did from superficial-seeming rave-bunnies. Now the miracle of sharing their love of ecstasy made the lovey-dovey rave sentiment real. Clubbing all comes down to ecstasy, I discovered. E was literally a cipher that explained the ravers' code, from their choice of kiddies' hair bobbles (ecstasy makes you nostalgic for childhood) to the repetitive music (there is no space for thought on ecstasy, only feelings, therefore music for e-heads is simple and unchallenging), to club motifs like pictures of a bomb with a lit fuse and a feather next to it (representing the rush and the sensuality that follows). It seemed to me now that anyone who was unfamiliar with the drug would be out of touch with the motivation behind raving. I kept taking quarter pills. The 'coolness' demanded of me by my ever-expanding circle of glistening and glamorous young urchin drug-buddies continued to be fazing. I always felt, and no doubt seemed, slightly alien to the whole scene, a little too cerebral and weird. Yet I was so proud to be one of them, one of the 'Children of the Rainbow', as one sect called itself. We all shared the ecstasy secret with teenage passion, striking out, destroying danger and temperance.

Around this time I became intensely nostalgic. At seventeen, it was the first opportunity to look back on childhood as a stage that was lost. It had been prompted by my flashback to the perceptions of a four-year-old in my first ecstasy trip. During those few seconds in which I felt as I had felt as a child, I had realized how much the wonder, love and innocence of infancy had corroded ever since. The flashback had been like a life flashing before my eyes on dying. Suddenly I found my entire childhood replete with dusty memories now fresh again at the fore of my thoughts. For months, I delved into those memories' exquisite poignancy, writing lists, compiling mental files of my tragic initiation into the 'prison-house' of social form.

> Trailing clouds of glory do we come
> From God, who is our home:
> Heaven lies about us in our infancy.

New memories came to me of my sister, Miriam, who was thirteen when I was born. How like a deity she had been to my amazed eyes all through my infancy. She had taken me for walks around Oxford's woolly brown fields to discuss 'fantasy' when I was only six, invented cakes and led fire-lit teenage dinner parties in nineteenth-century dresses or 1980s ballet clothes. I recalled my parents, how openly I had demanded and depended on them as a three-year-old, the way I had trusted them without reserve with my deepest spirit, as an infant ignorant of the fear that no-one could ever understand me. The freedom I had to ask any question without shame, the ebullience of my assumption that everyone was my friend . . . pathos and longing filled me for that self I had been – that unafraid, loving self. If I could in some small way recover part of that self, I felt, I could become confident and good in my adult life.

One day in my 'nursery' at Gran's – ironically this room had been my mother's as a child – I smoked a huge joint on my own. I had a vivid memory of being taught my ABCs at primary school aged five. Heading a page of my diary 'The Pure Voice', I let another self write to me:

ABCDEFGHIJKLMNOPQRSTUVWXYZ (They cheated me, they told me it was a song.) Uh I cried out loud the system is terrifying. IT'S REAL. But why and who? Am I just paranoid? God, the terror and the beauty.

It actually exists.

Above.

HEAVEN.

It is all description of grass, acid & e.

I see pictures of myself and I'm crying. It's so sad and yet so beautiful to cry. Why? I remember thinking that for the first time. I'm having FLASHBACKS to times when I was an infant and learning about the adult world, totally fresh and pure and being CORRUPTED. YES. It's true and it's making me cry. The way no-one escapes, it's fate. My heart's beating so hard in my chest I can feel it. I'm in another place, I'm running down labyrinths looking back over my shoulder.

'The best thing to do is to sit down together and see if you can work this thing out.'

You have to be brave to face this reality (get stoned) often. That's why I don't get stoned that much. I'm not brave. Remember learning the concept of brave?

It's a colourful, bright plastic jelly world. It's so sophisticated. You get drawn right into it. It moulds you like clay.

What is going on? The barrier always swings closed.

REMEMBER? Do you?

Too distanced to read – I feel preoccupied. First Sylvia Plath did not touch me, and nor did T. S. Eliot, and nor did the Bible.

I want a fairytale winter night. I know that they exist. I remember learning about them – the concept, not the experience. I never experienced it because I was born in England. Individuality

41

is that trivial. We are all the same really – or in a way – the system gets us in the same way. The system is just a neutral name for God.

It's got many sides.

It started when I saw – no, DID see – specks on my vision as if I was a camera or watching a film. Life was a picture, I was both watching and involved. I was waiting, sober, for the stoned, daring it not to come, but it suddenly came in that way.

Unbearable.

Bells ringing in country villages. Never saw that, I learnt it, but never saw it. I'm seeing those things. Things that you block out so much, things that have filled you so much, that you think they don't exist. Memories, flashbacks. Faces of others in hectic trip-form. Because the older you get, the more you slow down. I see things as this film. Like video pictures. Blurred images. Trance. It's a discovery. There are still things you discover, things you learn. But they are much fewer as you get older because you are so filled – there's only so much space or matter that is you. The world is made of jelly or bouncy rubber or coloured Plasticine and it exists? Does it? In a way.

A kind of bliss. You are naturally blissful as a person, Olivia. In this other reality, at least.

Then there is a gate that leads to the secret self. Admit it. Step out of the myth you learnt. Go on, do it if you really want to know the truth? Because rest assured there is a truth. You can relearn it if you want. Even though it's so painful and difficult to drop all the system that you learnt, to drop civilization, to drop all that is pretence, to live honestly – it's a different choice of life. People hate it. Only so very few people unlearn it. And yet you're here. Existential. Annoyingly pretentious. I am afraid I am. You could say it's a paranoia I've had since consciousness.

CONSCIOUSNESS.
I remember coming into consciousness. Being born into the system, being born at all. Everyone being born. Miracles. HOW STRANGE. Visions.

I feel pure again. I feel like a child again. Because I don't like the adult world. I'm odd. But only halfway there. I'm never sure if I'm, or how I'm, both mad and sane.

I'm standing at the barrier. And I'm going to go through the barrier, because of curiosity and indefinable WANTING TO. Remember learning that concept ('wanting to'). Reader – me – I feel I've been sent to you or anyway you MUST take my message. My message is being shown to me in images, because I have to or want to or CAN potentially understand it. Remember the word 'potentially'? I guess I was around eleven. What is a YEAR? Another thing you learnt. I'm skipping down a corridor kicking these ideas with my lace feet, merrily, lovingly, they're cotton toys and they're skittering over the floor. It's a fun thing to do . . . wait I'm doing it again . . . IDEAS. Messages.

A divine life. Everything is so profound, believe it. I want to talk to Lennon about TRUTH.

Sometimes I see a past life when I was a gypsy. A dark-haired little peasant gypsy woman in Eastern Europe. I'm afraid when people look into my eyes that they see this in me.

The wall is frustrating because you never know if it's just you or if everyone is together in this consciousness. You never know if any two people could possibly share one consciousness – it's something you refuse not to believe in. You push away feelings of aloneness. The first feeling of aloneness was when you were afraid of Miss Piggy on the Muppets and people laughed at you and asked why. She fascinated and terrified you. I'm giving you vital information

43

here, if you want to remember me. 'IES' = plural of 'Y'. Learnt that – I must have been four-five-six years old.

I visited heaven, conceived, experienced divine strength, joy. Nostalgia's embarrassing because it cuts you off. I feel so corrupted, so scared by what the system is & has done & will do to my soul. The world is dying, getting more and more corrupted and system-atized, and there's nothing you can do about it. But it's ok because the one thing you never really allow yourself to think about is death, what it is to die, and the sympathy cards in the shops. It's so fake, shadows of truth, what you usually perceive. It exists.

Trying to understand true, beautiful (because truth IS beauty) truth and infinity.

I only learnt that truth was beauty since taking e for the first time. That was what happened the first time that was so amazing: I understood that truth was beauty; beauty, truth. That was what e shows you. That's the previously indefinable quality of e. Why it made me feel conventional and fake and also why it makes me moved by the beauty of the truth I see, and makes me love beauti-ful things and see beauty everywhere, all the time, in every word spoken by anyone, in gestures of kindness – I respected and revered all beauty. The feeling was scary but beautiful. Everyone helps everyone else in the system. People you can't trust are people who won't help you. Groups of consciousness, islands made of wet yel-low mushy clay.

I remember such a happy time, so happy it's made me cry, suddenly overwhelmed with emotion. It caught me unaware. But but but when I remember this memory it's like imagining death. It is making me sob uncontrollably. I feel such sadness watching myself when I was little and innocent, before the world

44

corrupted me and the system corrupted me and most of all, ignor-
ant adults moulded and stuffed my pure soul with this plot,
before – God –

Crying releasing my shock and beautiful sadness but also terrify-
ing, alone, a child, pure again, knowing when I think of this trip I
won't ever understand it. I can just wish and hope.

I'm at the barrier.

I had been reading Coleridge's 'Frost at Midnight' before
smoking, and the poem's 'most believing . . . presageful' perceptions of 'The lovely shapes and sounds intelligible/Of that
eternal language, which thy God/Utters' had filled my mind,
especially his description of the spirit making 'a toy of
Thought' and his dreams of the timeless bells of his
birthplace.

The next day, I was disturbed by this outpouring. It was as if
a part of my unconscious had come to the surface and spoken
to me. I truly felt myself now to be at a barrier to knowledge; I
sensed my soul opening that gate. I felt a sense of incalculable
danger. I wrote soberly in my diary:

It is beautiful, painful and impossible. For the first time in my life
I feel these insights depressing me in a real way. Life just is impos-
sible in the face of all this awareness. If you want to know God,
there is no easy or simple way. I want to commune with God
directly, now I know God exists.

Reading these pieces now, some sober years later, I see things
that still seem true and things easily dismissed as tosh. I
am intrigued by the accuracy of the voice recording my

progression through a barrier and its warnings of the peril of deepening my exploration. I am struck by the naiveté of my dislike of civilization and my belief in all that drugs made me see and the religious element of my fantasies. It was hard at seventeen to question the basic message drugs impart, that their inspirations are true. Having taken ecstasy, I now saw God behind the system, no longer seperate from it as LSD had taught me.

The stoned mentor voice returned a few weeks later, when I wrote a prophetic entry in my diary under a title 'The Sermon'. Coleridge's mysterious, archetypal 'stranger' in 'Frost at Midnight', who could be

> Townsman or aunt, or sister more beloved,
> My play-mate when we both were clothed alike!

was at the forefront of my mind as I imagined this voice speaking to me as the stranger on the street – a divorced other self I had refused to recognize.

Stoned again. This is the most hectic time of my life. It's going to be my youth when I'm old. For once the present is more hectic than the flashback. Hello, I'm ALIVE! This is it, this is my life. Decisions, decisions. HECTIC. This is open to INFINITE – INFINITE – REALITY. If your mind is open to FOREVER, ETERNITY – then God is within you. My stoned sermon to myself:

You do not know how hectic your life is at the moment. You are changing and growing at hyper-speed. All the rest of your life, this will be your most hectic memory: this time. You are growing up, upwards. It's beautiful, don't be afraid. I am your soul, your eternal soul and your essence of God. Trust in me. Look up at the stars, the sea, the world, open yourself to it instead of being afraid to give yourself to it. The tragedy of your life is that you are restless and uneasy in your existence. I am on the other side of reality, and as you write now you are possessed by me, your connection with me is taut, strong and straight, as my light dawns. I am heaven, God, nirvana, ecstasy. I myself do not know or cannot explain to you what is going on with your unanswered question. Ask yourself what the question is before you expect me to answer, or my answer will never be seen to you. It is in my reactions, which you feel, but you do not know what you are looking for in me and so you are blinded and destroyed by my fragmentation. Is it moving to you to be open and therefore filled by me? You knew me whenever you saw me. But you were like the stranger on the street towards me. Lose all your inhibitions. You actually do not know how strange you are becoming. You might become 'insane'. It is a crisis. You can, however, rise above yourself and know that it's all ok. Build a statue, construct, create. Then you do something with and feel the reality of your existence. Except that it's also maybe just a dream, and everything is just random symbols. Most people go through life in this dream.

You are moving so fast you've lost your hold of your old perception of the past. You've stopped clinging to it, which is good, but difficult for you because you are becoming infinite, with life being less of a false, finite story. The past surprises you more, is more hectic and bigger, pregnant with a sweet disturbing truth.

Lennon remained sceptical of the rave circle, convinced it was pretentious, but he had never taken ecstasy, so his opinion was flawed. One day I turned up at his house with my oval, aerodynamic-style clubber sunglasses perched on my head and he was disappointed in me. I managed to reassure him I was not as shallow as I looked. To my parents' shock, my cousin Bobby threw me out of my Gran's house when he found out I had let Lennon stay in my room. The two of us moved in with Marc, who was house-sitting his sister's flat. We slept on a foam mattress on the living room floor and used newspaper for toilet tissue, wandered around in our underwear and argued laughingly over whose turn it was to play a song on the CD player. Marc and Lennon liked Radiohead, Led Zeppelin and obscure local rock bands, while I would insist on playing *Club Classics: Volume One.*

I did not know the name or artist of many of my favourite tunes, but my play-list of songs for my own ideal 'e tape' was:

'Transform' – Transformer
The song I came on to in Grahamstown
'Professional Widow' – Tori Amos
'That was Fantastic!'
'Sweet Baby'
Trance tape's best song – my favourite one
'Good Life' – Inner City
'Alex Party' – Alex Party
'Chime' – Orbital
'I Think We Should Get Back Together'
'G Marks the Spot' – Sensoria
'While Your Feet Are Stomping' – Scott Bond
'My Love is all Real'
'I'm Gonna be Free'

On a piece of paper decorated with butterfly stickers, in a large sloping hand, I recorded my ecstasy experience one night when we three had split a pill between us. I was on ecstasy when I wrote this:

Successions of images in a clear sequence. Actions, frozen or moving shots, in luminous colours against black chaos. Life and death. The movements are life. Repetition has utter beauty. Lights in the head. Great wonder. In the best moments, excited, feeling it's all a fantasy and you're just playing. Like a little child discovering fairies at the bottom of the garden. You re-experience belief, compassion and open-mindedness. Fun and games. Love, in a higher and more compassionate, selfless, objective dimension. Passion for crowds and tribes and groups – love for humanity. At the same time feeling selfish – acting selfish, feeling guilty because you are selfish. Like having an orgasm. As hectic as being very stoned – although e is much more intense, it is somehow familiar to dope – you can recognize it because no other drugs have it. You feel a bit helpless, like a child. Stupid (only, of course, in the terms of the adult world). Wishing sadly that others were on your level. You are very wise and see everything, but you don't feel a need to judge anything. A wonderful sense of aloneness, of exploring the world and people in front of you. Utter love for the people you feel are on the same level. Feeling on the edge, receptive, stubborn. Impersonal, part of the wonderful system. Ignorant and happy. Happy to make other people happy. Peace and wellbeing. Sunrises and sunsets flash in the mind. It feels like you're honoured to be alive. Nothing is denied, and everything is lovingly and gratefully received. You feel in a trance, it is painful to speak, music is all that matters because it trances you and satisfies your yearning. You

49

can depend on it. It also requires no effort: relaxation and luxury are needed. Reverence. Holiness. Icy shivers flash through you. It's slightly electric. Like standing looking up into a night sky when it's snowing. That sense of wonder and discovery. Like a princess in a playground. Having to have your own space. Deeply absorbed and fascinated by the feeling. Helpless again. A stray sober thought wanders in viciously. Disappointment fighting excitement. Deep yearning, strong emotions. Calm, soothing music reassures you. It repeats itself, it's dependable, it's predictable; it tells you every-thing's ok. It's in the void but is an expression of it, so you can feel it, but when you're in the void without any guidance or expression to help you, you're lost. Because the actuality of the void, truth, God, whatever, is 100 percent beyond human conception. So there's no need to try to comprehend it. You shield your eyes from it as you do from the sun. You are quiet. You are happy to be resigned to life.

Cartoons. Jokes. Fun. Holding a torch aloft, firing an arrow into the sky, leaping into the colours of the sunset. Such happiness. Chain-smoking. Lengthiness. Eternal images and classic actions fit the e mould. Great need for love, pure and generous and selfless love, to be given to you. Slight sorrow that beats on the door of your mind. Constant calm. You live only for pleasure. Intrinsic good in everything. Wanting to take some more. No hunger. Spiritual energy, like a deep well. Appreciating things. Creativity flowing out of you. Able to be kind, to be positive. High. Close to tears. Massive objectivity and feeling of being God. Contempt for speech. The tongue simply would not be able to bear beating against the inside of your mouth. It is impossible to do anything so nasty. Too comfortable to move, or too lazy. A feeling of dying as you come down. Pickled in honey. Unsure. Knowing nothing matters but afraid that it might, you might have to care. A 'what happened?' dazed feeling drenches you drop by drop. Also relief after a while. Farewell.

The following day I realized that the experience had not been as blissful as before. This was exemplified by writing while high. It had been a more thoughtful, less abandoned, experience. But still exciting in its atavism, the emotion of communion with the essence of human nature. I had sensed the ruthless implacability and permanence of the human race, had felt my own place in this fit survival. The ecstasy-driven emotion was one of proud contentment to be part of this great achievement, humanity, satisfaction in my human ignorance of greater mysteries and pleasure in all humane behaviour. Ecstasy was being human, living sheltered in an enclosed world of *things*. It was about the joy and virtue of action rather than thought or exploration. 'Ours is not to reason why, ours is but to do and die.' I had always been opposed to this, a critic of convention. Now, here I was, celebrating the disingenuous harmony of society.

At school I had been teased for being gullible. When he was in a cynical mood, Lennon sometimes said that the reason he fell in love with me was because I was so impressionable. I couldn't be sarcastic to save my life. I believed most of what I was told. I took perverse pride in cultivating my open-mindedness, making a motto for myself that I would rather be a fool than cynical, but really I had no option in the matter. It did not cross my consciousness to question the thoughts that came into my head when I was on drugs. There was a conflict emerging between the pervasive trust reinforced all around me, in people I knew and in the media, in ecstasy as the harmless love drug, and my own almost shameful suspicion I had not yet articulated, that something about that love rang false.

I wanted to explore religion. My immediate family was not religious, but Gran was a lifelong Bible scholar and poet with a strong mystical apprehension, and my grandfather had been a rabbi, though more as a living than a calling. Perhaps some of Gran's religious genes passed down to me. Yet the mystical scene in my life, that of drugs, was curiously hollow. The South African version of clubbing had a particular falseness in its racial exclusiveness. It drew only the white, wealthy segment of society. Compared to England, middle-class life in South Africa was removed from reality: it was provincial, undemanding, a place where no-one read books and international news was barely reported. The culture of middle-class people seemed emptied out by apartheid, a bland replica of a fictitious America. How could an educated English girl search for religion in such a society? I mentally separated mass rave culture from my growing group of adventurous friends, and preferred to take drugs in nature or at home with people I loved. Yet I was still awed by the glamorous, mindless side of ecstasy, which inexplicably, a law unto itself, seemed a natural fit with the empty smoothness of white South Africa.

One fine night in August, Lennon, Marc and I decided to try smoking ecstasy. We crumbled up half a pill in some Swaziland grass, rolled it up and passed it between us. I remember us being out of our minds, lolling between doorframes, and the rest is blank. On other nights we would go out in a bigger group and some of us would share some pills. My search for that original high was all-encompassing: ecstasy had affected my soul, unlike any other drug. The only thing to which it took second place was my worship of Lennon. I managed to arrange work experience for myself at *Elegance*, a South African women's magazine, and I would go in after a night on the town and fall asleep in the back room of the fashion department.

14 August 1996

Dear Grace,

Thank you for your wonderful, witty, funny, sweet, beautiful letter. I miss you sooooo much.

Sorry I haven't written for so long. Life . . . well, it's been unbelievably hectic. I haven't had a single moment to think on my own for the last four days. I'm grabbing this time to write to you during my lunch break.

So anyway, I'm at Elegance doing . . . guess what? . . . FASH-ION! I'm actually working eight hours a day in an office crammed with Grace-friendly stuff: back issues of every international fashion magazine, hundreds of designer clothes. In a way I wish it was you here instead of me, because I know that, for every bit of appreciation I have for all the fashion eight hours a day, you would appreciate it infinitely more. To me, sometimes it gets a bit much – the fuss that is made over a single tiny photograph of a shoe astounds (& distresses!) me.

I wonder very much how you are & where exactly you are. I really hope you are happy.

My two great passions at the moment are 1) Lennon and 2) pool. No, make that three: 3) ecstasy. I took it again on

Saturday & it was much less intense than the first time, far more serene & mellow. We went to a club called The Boiler Room where they play British disco house – wonderful music. At about 4 or 5 a.m. we went on to a rave in a warehousy building where the atmosphere was better. I don't like the pretension of clubs; I am starting to prefer warehousy places where there's more space & reality & fewer fashion victims & more real ravers.

Some things are worrying me. I'm hardly aware of them due to the hecticness of life but that in itself worries me. For ages now I've been in a kind of mist – I mean, living so entirely in each moment that I can't remember stuff, even what happened forty-eight hours ago, let alone last week. I never think objectively about what I'm doing anymore.

I have been spending a lot of my time getting stoned: consequently my life changes at hyper-speed. I feel myself changing; maybe I'm growing up. I am learning so much I never understood before.

I'm going to a rave in the Karoo. I have a feeling it's going to be a memorable weekend.

On Saturday Marc, Cara, her mate Merlin, Anne, Jen, Pete, Gary and I went to an 'unofficial' trance party in the countryside by the coast. We drove one and a half hours each way and it was in the middle of nowhere. We were so stoned, it felt amazing to be in nature. The party had tee-pees and a fire and a hippy selling weed and we all smoked his bong.

I'm getting seriously addicted to drugs – always craving e. When I take e I am so happy that normal life just can't compare. I get more and more into house, trance, etc. e has changed me so much: it taught me that 'truth is beauty, beauty truth'.

I miss you, miss you, miss you. I am sorry that this letter is so bitty, and that when I do have time to write, as now, I'm too tired and spaced out to write properly.

Take care. I miss you!

All my love,

Olivia

Chapter Three

We left for Verneukpan (Deceiving Pan, because of the continuous circular mirage that gives the impression it is an island)
on a Thursday evening, a whole contingent of ravers together
on an old coach. I had made friends with my companion Alice
on the train to the southern suburbs as we went home from
work each day. She had been to school with Lennon and Marc,
one of the only non-white children in their experimental
school during the pre-Mandela nineties. Her father was African, her mother Asian, and they were well off. This gave Alice
access both to the rich liberal white community and the rough
gangland suburbs of the Cape flats on whose outskirts she
lived. The two of us loved to laze around smoking spliffs,
talking about the soul's progress and watching corny talk
shows on television. She was comfortable and easy going, and
we had agreed to share a tent at the four-night rave.

Accompanying her were Bronwen and Betty, two girls I had
never met. Bronwen was dressed entirely in red and had dyed
her bobbed hair scarlet. Betty had done the same thing with
blue. Her crew-cut, accentuated by royal blue dye, appeared
to me seriously tough. At eighteen they were, or portrayed
themselves as, hardcore ravers. Neither showed any sign of

friendliness, but Betty in particular took an instant dislike to me. She looked at me suspiciously, as if to say, 'you're not one of us'. My heart sank thinking of the weekend ahead. I missed Lennon already. As the coach rolled away from Cape Town and the spliffs were passed around, music pumping on the in-coach stereo, I opened a love letter from him. It was the most intimate letter I had ever received and I lived in its world in my mind for the rest of the night-long drive.

When we arrived in the saltpan, the dawn was dazzling. Disorientated by the unrelenting emptiness, we pitched our tents. The sun beat down like nothing I had ever felt before on the table-flat white sheet of ground, sizzling off it. It felt like being adrift on an ice rink without edges. There was nothing much to do but wait for sunset. I took a shower in the communal washing area and felt the weird sensation of my hair drying almost within seconds. It was obvious why people didn't live in such an environment. It was unspeakably harsh. Too hot to do anything while the sun was up but sit under a sheet drinking fluids and gazing around at the vast panorama with awe. When evening came, the temperature dropped to freezing as the most enormous full moon I had ever seen rose to dominate the black sky. It had its own dawn, seeming half as big as the sun and emitting strong beams of light. It seemed unshakeably as though the landscape was watching us. There were millions of days and nights the saltpan had had of such sun and such moons, year after year, unseen by human or animal. What must it think of us tiny, crude little ants camping on a fraction of its inhumane surface?

I was unhappy, not sure whether it was some mood of my own, the unfriendliness of Bronwen and Betty, or due to the landscape, so wrenchingly unfamiliar and, above all, without an exit. I could not quite enjoy it.

In our tent in this desert, we sat on sleeping bags on the floor. A madly smiley, tanned young man rolled up a carrot spliff, followed by a giant one in the shape of a flower, which we all smoked. The atmosphere was intense. To my surprise, it was only 6.30 in the evening when people started getting ready for their drug supper: es and sweets. Mandy passed around the pills. I ended up passively accepting a whole white tablet and saying I would only suck half of it. Most of the others took their whole pills. Alice took her first ever tab of acid, also whole, which I thought was daring. When I was halfway through my pill, I wondered if I should stick to my words. Of course I was not yet experiencing anything. I felt fine and thought, 'I haven't tried a whole one yet, maybe now's the time.' Slightly ill at ease from the strong, pure skunk spliffs and the self-consciousness induced by sitting in a large circle of strangers huddled in one space in a vast empty desert, I did not want to draw attention to how little I was taking by saying I could not finish it. I started to worry and then reminded myself of the Zen wisdom we always tried to follow: 'Let it be. Accept. Relax.' It became the vernacular of e: 'Just relax, don't worry, don't think, everything is fine.' So I let the rest dissolve in my mouth.

Still sober, everyone decided to go to 'come on' at the rave's stage. As we approached out of the dark night, stumbling across flat, white earth, I spotted the chill-out tent and sensed it was a nicer place to be. An acquaintance, Max, was there, sitting on a cushion on the huge piles of customized rags and beckoning me over. I felt the happiness of welcome. As I walked towards him, I felt the rush come on with a moment of joy. The world was graceful. He was. I was. In this peace everything could just slow down and become infinitely more intense. I felt my teeth go into a rictus smile. Was this good? Then suddenly I was drowning in a tsunami. It was a rush, but more than a rush. I was burning up. My heart was bursting, accelerating, I couldn't walk, my breath became one long inhalation – as I tried to submit and go with the flow – until I couldn't breathe anymore. *Is this the same rush everyone raves for and about? I don't like it.* My horizon went black and at the same time threads of different colours shot like electricity in my head. I thought I was about to faint. Max helped me out of the tent, supporting me concernedly. He guided me to a dark spot just to the side of the stage and stood aside as I threw up on the empty ground.

After throwing up the contents of my stomach, I felt I must have got most of it out of my system. This was impossible, but perhaps it was enough to believe it. The panic faded and I was left indifferent and washed out. I no longer cared. I had been through the worst. A bomb had ripped through me and all that was left was a pliable, sensate piece of Plasticine for the massive forces of the mind and universe. Mind and universe being one and the same thing, inner-being outer, like a Möbius strip or a yin-yang symbol. I felt fine again, relieved as though I had been crying and now was realizing life was not that bad.

I guess that's why Mandy said you feel like you need to be hospitalized, I thought. Suddenly I started rambling, trying to get Max into a conversation about the universe and the rave. I was recovering much too fast to be in my right mind; I was too stressed and was bringing him down. He excused himself and made his way off. I was hurt, but understandably, perhaps, he thought I was a freak for responding in this way to the drug. This just did not happen to people all that often. Perhaps just once or twice in a crowded night. He was sweet but conventional. It was not considered feminine to throw up on drugs. Especially so violently.

No matter. I wandered around, met up with Alice, who said she needed me as much as I needed her, and we went back to our tent. Some others came along too and we read my tarot cards. I was reading tarot as if inspired. I felt I was channelling the insights of God, able to speak more clearly and accurately than I ever could sober. Then we were alone again and two strange young men came and sat with us for a while. We got nervous of them. Alice said she was going to get water and I was left alone with them. I told them it was nice meeting them but I was going to go and accompany Alice now, so they had to leave. Relieved to escape them, I caught up with Alice and we walked out to the water tent together. It was about a ten-minute walk across the empty, lunar landscape dotted with tents. The lasers, unobstructed, swept for miles across the earth, as far as the eye could see. They drew shapes and designs on the black horizon in time with the music. We looked at the stars and thought we saw a flying saucer. We willed it to land and thought maybe it had. We were both happy and safe in each other's company and we felt like survivors. Then a long walk back, and as the drugs wore off, a long night and dawn chilling out and coming down. I was relieved to be leaving that day.

Soon after dawn, Alice and I packed up our tent and back-packs and repositioned ourselves at the main tent to await the

9 a.m. bus to return us to Cape Town. All around us, cars full of multinational über-ravers sped away and shaven-headed, tattooed organizers dismantled stages and electrical equipment. Soon there were only twenty-five of us left in the whole desert, waiting under a sheet for the bus. We scanned the empty horizon. It was late. The sun rose to its peak at noon in pulsating silence. We lay exhausted on our backs, murmuring about the cool drinks and salad we would eat when we got home. I was starting to question if we ever would get out. Was the bus lost? How was it supposed to find us in the first place? Food was running short. We discussed the possibility of helicopter rescue. Someone managed to contact one of the rave organizers by phone, who was dismayed to hear we were still waiting for the errant bus. As the day ground on, it emerged that the bus driver was indeed lost, and that another bus had been dispatched from the nearest remote town, Kenhardt. Early in the evening, we spotted the bus on the horizon, weaving its way towards us. It then vanished from sight, lost in the identikit landscape. Finally it reappeared and the driver noticed our frantic waving. An ancient brown school bus with wooden seats, it screeched to a halt in a cloud of dust.

The overnight journey home seemed endless to me. I had turned inwards, but everyone else woke up renewed for more partying.

'Anyone got any good house?' a boy whooped as soon as we had boarded.

'Olivia's got!' called out Alice. 'Come on, isn't there that one in your Walkman?' she asked me.

Bizarrely, I had been the only raver to bring along a tape of house music. The tape, a mix by DJ Tony de Vit, immediately poured out down the length of the rickety bus. The next thing I knew, Bronwen had taken her top off and was sitting cross-legged in the aisle snorting a ground-up pill. The boys loved it. Soon half the passengers in the bus were cavorting half naked snorting anything in sight. The driver didn't know what to do.

'I've got a big apple for sale,' announced the boy sitting behind me.

I bought the pill from him. He gave it to me in a matchbox.

We stopped for refreshment at a tiny rural town after six hours on the road. We hijacked its empty little bar-come-general store, putting my tape on the loudspeakers and starting up a dance floor. I felt sorry for the owners and wondered how they would clean up afterwards, but I danced half-heartedly anyway.

'We've brought them a rave!' Bronwen squealed in her bra, while Betty jerked around dancing moodily. 'They'll never forget us! They love us!'

Back in the bus the party kept going right up until we reached the grey, wintry northern suburbs of Cape Town in the morning rush hour. Gradually everyone slumped as best they could, the wooden seats now unforgivingly hard.

7 October 1996

Dear Grace,

So good to hear from you. You asked what was happening – so here we go:

My life recently seemed to reach some kind of intense, scary climax. This is what happened the last month or so . . .

I started smoking more and more grass, and having some very emotional realizations, & the more I smoked, the more insecure & confused I got – confused about who 'I' am. Then not last weekend but the one before I had the worst weekend – the most surreal, freaked out, lonely weekend. I was at the rave in the Karoo. I don't know quite how to explain it. I haven't even fully understood it myself yet. I left on the Thursday night, on a mad coach of ravers & weirdos. Having driven & smoked grass throughout the night to a soundtrack of hard trance music, we arrived on the Friday morning in <u>THE DESERT</u>. I can not tell you how weird the place was. Basically it was a saltpan – i.e. the moon. The ground was COMPLETELY flat, like cracked hard clay. The horizon surrounded us 360 degrees, and so it felt like being in a continuous circle. The horizon was also a continuous mirage, since the saltpan was 30 x 60 km (huge). So it looked like the circle was bordered by a circular ocean. There was no escape from this never-ending emptiness. It was absolutely desolate – no animals, insects or blades of grass. The sun was like no sun I've ever known. It was so relentlessly hot that at times you felt unable to breathe. I was with people I hardly knew & felt more alone & trapped than I had ever conceived of before. I was in this place for four days. Not a moment alone, no place to go, too hot to sleep or to eat the days away.

To make things worse, everyone was on drugs, so you couldn't connect with anyone on a normal level. Do you know what it is like to be in a desert with 1000 people all of whom are tripping off their faces? I was feeling unable to cope socially! It felt like endless small-talk, trying so hard to be cool & relaxed & happy like the people on e when all I wanted was to die.

On the Saturday night I took my first whole e – it lifted me out of my depression for three or four hours – then I came down.

I just got more & more freaked out & felt like the walking dead.

The worst thing was that I had nowhere to go to be alone, to escape the desert & the people who were scaring me so badly. It was impossible to stray from the tents because it was too hot to leave their shade.

Then, on the day we were meant to return to CT, the bus never came. The other ravers all left, the whole rave was packed away, but for us twenty to thirty people waiting for the coach. At that point I thought I was fated to die right there. Finally the rave organizers found a school bus to drive us home. The trip home took thirteen hours. The driver didn't even know where Cape Town was.

I have never been so happy to lie in a cool room in a bed and drink mineral water as I was last week.

It took the experience in the desert to show me a more negative side of ravers. I realized that it is one thing to go to a rave for one night, but when I spent time with e-heads, I found that a) I soon couldn't cope with it because a lot of them (in South Africa, anyway) are totally superficial, and b) I am not a person who is into drugs and raving for days on end like that.

The one good part of the weekend was that I made a close friend in the girl I shared a tent with, Alice. She was really kind and nice to me when I was depressed – she is a deep, caring person. The night I e'd, she took her first whole acid trip, and we spent our trips together, which was actually a brilliant experience.

Last night I went to Alice's twenty-first birthday party. I wish you could meet her. Lennon & I shared an e, punch and a few spliffs – he had his first real e experience, and was uncharacteristically confident, whereas for me, the e trips seem to get worse rather than better (I've decided not to do it so often). It made me very nervy last night, which was why I drank, to mellow it out – and soon felt great. It was a house party, & the house & garden were filled with Alice's friends and relatives. I met loads of people.

I am daily more in love with Lennon.

I seem to be forgetting more & more about England. The only slang I remember is 'mate', 'wicked' and 'draw'. Lennon and I are currently into talking like the Fugees. We tell people 'it's time to settle the score', etc. Anyway please tell me what's going on in the world. I feel so cut off (no radio/TV/newspapers since June!!) All I read here is You *magazine, like a unisex* Women's Own *with headlines such as 'Five cent coin stuck in Erina's intestines for four years'. I kid you not.*

I feel slightly depressed these days – probably a result of:

a) lying around too much;

b) too many stupid drugs (I really mean this. When I e'd in the Karoo I threw up before it took normal effect. I'm sick of drugs, I really am. A buzz is all too predictable in a way.); and

c) Greater awareness – life is no longer defined for me. It's infinite, terrifying. I feel lost, unable to connect with people, too real for happiness.

Help . . . oh, maybe I just need a good stiff drink or ten. Or maybe I should get out more.

Oh well . . . I miss you and long for you!

Write soon.

All my love,

Olivia

Suddenly I realized I had inadvertently stumbled across one of the classic themes of poetry, the moral relationship between truth and beauty. I was living the tragic divorce of these two ways. In an ideal world, I theorized, such as the world as experienced by an infant, or heaven, or indeed my first ecstasy trip, truth and beauty were one and the same. Being honest would never hurt anyone, since candour would be graceful, the truth would be beautiful. All, absolutely all, the insecure shame people hide inside, that they fear makes them unlovable, was in fact beauty. Ecstasy taught me this, that there was nothing to conceal, no thought or feeling that was evil and unredeemable. All honest feelings were, in that loved-up ideal state, good.

In the same way, beauty had to be true. From this angle the equation was harder to believe, because I instinctively felt that aesthetic concerns were superficial and false. I had spent my teenage years raging against society's obsession with meretricious appearances. Yet the beauty that I eventually saw and felt when I was on ecstasy was honest and ethical. It was the kind of real beauty you see when you lovingly recognize the good character of a friend. It was not just that charming thoughts were true. It was more that anything legitimately beautiful was true. Not falsely beautiful, like people flaunting designer clothes and plastic surgery, or sweet but meaningless speeches full of lies, but things with inner beauty. Poetry, art, music, nature, dance.

One stoned night in September, while still happy and almost nostalgically in thrall of ecstasy, I had imagined e-beauty as a human character and then written a metaphorical account of my first time on ecstasy as a meeting with the following protagonist:

Standing in the classroom or the playground, he had (it is more infinitely beautiful than you, the reader, can conceive of) lived in an unremembered way, drawn to the ideas which only tug at the hearts of normal people. He wept as a child and also as an adult – he did not cry; he wept, like a weeping willow draped in snow in an infant's meadow. To others he was fascinating and dangerous, and he was much desired, by many romantic, modern women.

I have known him all my life. One night under the stars, at a time when I was not feeling too unhappy – that is, I was feeling happy – I was standing looking up at the sky, watching its beauty vibrate overhead, when he told me he loved me.

It was a night I never forgot.

It was of a nature impossible to forget. Nobody who has felt what I felt in that moment can ever . . . But I must not justify myself . . . I must not get paranoid. I felt that I was like him and that he was like me: we included each other – we formed a whole together. The thing I realized that night, that I never realised before, was so infinite that I can not describe it.

Ecstasy, or love, had unified truth and beauty in this way for me. Now for some reason I was depressed and everything was inverted. The truth was ugly and beauty was a lie.

What bothered me was that these days, each time I took a pill, the high was getting less glorious, and that beauty which had been so completely assured, which I had been so relieved to trust having been eluded by it my whole life, started to seem just a little bit plastic. 'Plastic' was the only word for it. I'd be on e, in my favourite clubs, dancing, aspiring to feel that original ecstasy feeling again, but instead there would be a tinge of desperation and mediocrity. No matter how I tried to make my dance unique, I couldn't help but notice that on ecstasy I was only capable of dancing like a robot. As with 'plastic', there was no escape from that word: 'robot'. It made my Ndancing more demure and graceful but it was not me. My smile and those of others seemed falsely fixed. So joyful from the outside, concealing an unspeakable fear of failing to be ecstatic on the inside. Our jaws were tensed, grinding hectically. Flowers and other decorations and even people looked, at times, as if they were literally made out of plastic. Expressions of emotion felt showy even as I gave them voice. I could not find anything genuine – all my raw emotions were sublimated into a fashionable, homogenous chemical smoothness and sweetness by the drug. None of this would have been at all disturbing, had not the drug been known to me and the rest of my generation as the drug of 'love'. Now either the pills were of a lower quality than during that first wonderful vanilla cream in June, or ecstasy, which had become fatally entwined with love and God in my mind, was not quite right. Beauty was no longer exactly true. Looking back, the perfection of even the first few moments on e seemed too intense to be supported for more than a few minutes, so the idea of such perfection being eternal heaven felt overwhelming.

Yet at this stage I was so obsessed with the world of good beauty which the first pill had opened up that I tried to interpret my new, worse e trips as part of the same heavenly realization. Plasticity and roboticism were now, by sole dint of their association with my god, e, to become holy perceptions to me. This went against every natural and educated instinct I had, but, like a religious fanatic who takes up violence in God's name, I was willing to accept these flaws in 'god' in order to hold onto 'god' as a whole.

I wrote a poem at this time expressing the whole disturbing problem:

I Believe in Beauty

Acknowledge your cynicism,
Dream your conception,
Smoke your cigarettes till dawn,
See the pain outside your eyes,
Lack when you lack,
Smile when you're born.
These echo the steps of fear,
Bouncing along the path of knowledge,
Looking there, and glancing here,
Pouncing on each other, solid.
I can not shut my eyes to this,
Victorian I am in this.
This, why, this is my descent and my arrival.
Its energy is mine: it gives to me,
And, terribly, I do not give to it,
Because I am a little girl, afraid of it,
I deny the source; in another way:
'Good morning passengers, my name is Glamour,
I'm gonna take you up to the stars,
And show you all that is beautiful
– Yet somewhere false and cruel –
And I will then evade you when you doubt me.
I'm plastic, and I'm fast –'

And I slip away as you kill me with your beauty,
Since now, come, we know beauty is life and death,
And let us not break the struggle of every bloody day,
And we will hide and hibernate our selves,
And cover them with human breath.

Most people I knew who took drugs did not take them at all seriously. They used the drugs to party and never listened to what the drugs told them for any longer than the time they were high. The night after I first had a plastic moment on ecstasy, I was at Cara's house and asked her if she recognized that feeling from her own ecstasy experience. In fact her only ecstasy trip had been under tragic circumstances, so I would not have expected her to have had a good trip. About a year before, when she was seventeen, she had been invited out by a twenty-five-year-old, Robert. He had taken her to a bar where they had shared a few drinks. Suddenly she was falling madly in love with him. She had never felt anything like it. Was this what people meant when they said, 'You know when it's love'? The force of the emotion sweeping her was incredible. She found herself telling Robert she loved him. He laughed. 'So you like it then!' he said.

'What do you mean?'

'Shall we pop another?'

It all fell into place. He had spiked her drink.

'What is it? What did you put in my drink?'

'Chill out, it's only a pill. You were enjoying it, why the stress?'

She got up and called a taxi. It took her a week to recover enough from this mind-bending trip to see that she had not fallen in love with him. She had never wanted to take drugs, and was now put off even more.

Yet when I asked her to describe the high, she said it had been good and that she had, like me, seen things as plastic. It had not crossed her mind to question the co-existence of a good trip with seeing things as plastic, in other words, as false and man-made. My mind insisted on understanding these drugged thoughts, incorporating them into my daily con- sciousness. This was partly my natural way, and partly the influence of Lennon and Marc, who had for several years been taking drugs, particularly LSD, as a philosophical adventure. Once Lennon told me how he had had an overwhelmingly bad acid trip. For days following it, he was unable to resolve what- ever it was he had learned on that trip. His solution, amalgam- ated from Blake, Huxley and the Doors, was that once the doors of perception have been cleansed, there is no going back. Only by going further could he resolve his problem, so he overcame his terror of the drug and took it once more and somehow managed to work through the situation. He survived sober and unscathed.

Our days were full of the works of Carlos Castaneda and Jung's *Memories, Dreams, Reflections* – books that took the 'spiritual' seriously. Nights were spent stoned at one another's houses or in Cape Town's bars, clubs, raves and outdoor festi- vals. I was happy: in love with Lennon, surrounded by friends, full of ideas and exploratory desires. We would smoke vast amounts of Swazi brick or Durban Poison, discuss philo- sophical insights, drive to the movies or dress up and improvise films with a video camera. When Halloween that year, 1996, came, we went to a party in fancy dress at The Fringe, Cape

Town's veteran alternative club, which later burnt down. The Fringe, with its outdoor smoking 'pit', cabal of grungy surfer dudes and 'hectic' music like Hole and The Pixies, had been our favourite club the year before. Now we spent more time in house and trance clubs, but retained a nostalgic love of The Fringe. That Halloween night was a disturbing one for me. I recorded it the next day in my diary.

Some hectically strange stuff happened at The Fringe last night, and I have realized various things about reality and drugs. Before we left, we ate space cakes [cakes baked with marijuana]. I only had a few bites, but my stomach was empty and it hit like LSD. And I had a bad trip. A really bad, terrifying, horrific trip. It's quite painful to remember it but I want to record it. We went to The Fringe, I was fine. As the car stops as we get there, I get out and suddenly I'm tripping off my face. I feel full of emotion. This friend of someone's, Caroline, is being really bitchy to me and has been all night, I'm suddenly full of potential anger. She pushes rudely past me and before I know what I'm doing I push her back. As soon as I've done it, I am possessed by terrible guilt and I feel as if I lost control. I tell Lennon I have to talk to him, I suddenly feel hopelessly depressed and in need of him. We go into The Fringe and everything and everyone is unspeakably terrible. It is as if I have become sensitive to every little thing. Everyone seems to be contemptuous of me. Over and over again, I get hurt. I can't believe how everything is going sour and wrong. I am just possessed by this terrible feeling and it's getting bigger. We sit in the pit and I am totally isolated from everyone around me. The force of depression just possesses me utterly. Lennon is being really nice to me but everyone else is lost to me. I am terrified. Suddenly I can't help but

73

surrender to the feeling, and I feel myself go over the edge. I just feel this knowledge of evil. I know that life is evil and horrific. I know everything. I cry on Lennon's shoulder, feeling in infinity, real, beautiful and inexpressibly miserable. Lennon takes me to the car. I am hallucinating off my head. As we sit down in the car I feel like I'm calming down. Then suddenly everything is catapulted back into the WORST HORROR I HAVE EVER KNOWN. I just don't know how to describe it. The basic thing I was aware of was that the devil was with me, or trying to get through to me. Fearful images from deep in my subconscious suddenly appeared to me. I recognized each one from memory. They were the images that have been in my worst nightmares and most private consciousness from infancy. Utterly obscure and yet utterly real in those moments. My subconscious fears all came into visual consciousness. In those moments I knew everything. I was confronted with my real self and its childhood terrors. It was torture. I looked at Lennon's face – which was made up for the Halloween party – it wasn't Lennon's face. It was all my worst nightmares come true. It was Pennywise the clown from IT, grinning at me. It was the suicidal Nijinsky smiling horrifically at me. All I knew was that the devil was appearing to me. The crisis was worse because Lennon is my love. It was like the fear I used to have that my mother and Miss Piggy from the Muppets were one. The horror was unspeakable, absurd. I was in total terror. At the same time, Lennon was trying to talk to me and comfort me and being really himself and nice, but I didn't know if he was the devil or not. One second I'd know he was Lennon and the next he was the devil. Then a dream I had about a year ago came into my mind. In the dream, my father had been possessed by Lennon and had murdered me. The fear of it lay in the fact that I trust my father and Lennon above all others. The dream, therefore, had a horrible irony, a devilishness. As the dream came into my head, I realized that (cosmically) I trust and love the very idea that wants to destroy me. I thought, 'My real self is trying to find the devil. It wants to be killed by the devil.' As Lennon looked at me and stroked me, I knew he was the devil but the only way I could please the devil and save myself was to have sex with the devil. I thought, I search for all the things that terrify me most. I want to consummate my terror with the devil. That is my destiny. I thought, Lennon is so familiar. I have been with him in my past lives. I want to make it clear that it wasn't that I thought Lennon WAS the devil. I knew Lennon (the real Lennon) was good. But I thought the devil was appearing in Lennon's face to show me the utter horror of the person you love and trust being the subconscious terror you've had in dreams your whole life. I felt that the devil was trying to scare me into psychosis. I rubbed the make-up off Lennon's face so he looked himself again. Then I came back to reality.

I just don't want to go any further into knowledge.

Lennon was so good to me that I almost feel that he won that battle with the devil. I feel kind of guilty and bad that the devil appeared in his face. But I never thought he was the devil. As I have said, it was the devil trying to trick me, corrupt, destroy love.

I've now realized that, although there is an infinite reality, I am not prepared to go into it any further. I am literally unprepared and helpless in it. I would rather live ignorant and happy. And now that I've written all that horror down, I am just going to forget it as best I can.

By the next day, I was back to writing my usual giggly entries in my diary. In retrospect, this was a natural teenage yearning for cosmic exploration. I had not yet developed the power to turn my back on frightening or outrageous ideas, as I learnt to as an adult. If something terrible or wonderful suggested itself to me, like the idea of the devil wanting my soul, or visiting heaven, I dove into the idea. There were limits of sanity I would never cross: I would never have dreamed of following my mind into hurting anyone else or myself; if thoughts about causing damage had come to my mind, they would have been dismissed with concern. Rather, my disturbing thoughts questioned the boundaries of existence.

As such, it seemed right to explore 'spirituality'. Inspired by Carlos Castaneda, I saw drugs as a route to knowledge and, without my own shaman to guide me, took rather too lightly the metaphysical peril of knowing what is normally hidden, of developing powers of awareness too great to control. In Jung's *Memories, Dreams, Reflections,* in the chapter titled 'Confrontation with the Unconscious', Jung wrote: 'This is the fund of unconscious images which fatally confuse the mental patient. But it is also the matrix of a mythopoeic imagination which has vanished from our rational age. Though such imagination is present everywhere, it is both tabooed and dreaded, so that it even appears to be a risky experiment or a questionable adventure to entrust oneself to the uncertain path that leads into the depths of the unconscious.' Reading the book at the time, I did not take this as an encouragement to follow this 'uncertain path', but was grateful for his understanding of the fine to non-existent line separating the exploration of the unconscious with mental illness. I felt entirely sane. There was nothing impeding my ability to think; in fact my brain was never more honed than at the height of my worries, excess worry being a sign of an overactive mind craving application. Jung comprehended the need for mythical, serious imagination, for true adventure, missing in modern life and exhaustively sought by the young.

Drugs do not distort reality: they are reality. Life is simply a 3D, physical enactment of infinitely greater (!!*!)*, I wrote in my diary two weeks before my breakdown began. I spent my eighteenth birthday like every other day that South African spring, getting stoned with Lennon, listening to Kate Bush singing 'Wuthering Heights' and thereby reliving the innocence of infancy that song had recalled when I first took ecstasy. I wrote in my diary, *I picture myself at home, beautiful November rain and darkness, days so grey I never notice them, tall white rooms, and red sun burning and dying in the ethereal mist. Me reading. The living room decorated for a party. The kitchen decorated too. I wear my best dress. In my smile is excitement. The rooms are lit up. How I long for someone to tell me everything is ok and I am safe. Someone to tell me my depression is – what is it? – homesickness? – cosmic consciousness? – mental illness? – trauma? – madness? – at least – conceivable to society. Someone to tell me I'm part of society.*

My nostalgia for childhood and home knew no bounds. I felt that as a child and on that original ecstasy trip, I had been able to be honest, happy, excited and popular whereas now I was alienated from everyone except my closest friends, unable to communicate my real thoughts in case people found them weird. I hibernated and spent more time alone with Lennon. I kept telling myself to go out and 'be yourself' but was too paranoid. I wondered if ecstasy had shown me a glimpse of heaven and then taken it away, if it was impossible ever to feel truly happy again.

What I called depression at this time was nothing compared to what I was about to undergo. It was a serious sense of unease, which was not surprising considering the moments I had had in the saltpan and on Halloween. A more sensible girl would have taken this feeling as a warning and quit drugs there and then. But it was underpinned by a softness and sweetness, a harking back to lost days of perfection when I was a child and a few months before, when ecstasy had shown me 'paradise'. Happiness existed as a past and a future. I did not know the meaning of depression.

Then at the beginning of December, my mood cheered. I decided to stop being afraid and just be myself, as self-help books said. I decided, fatally, that blaming ecstasy for my moods was just a red herring and that I could e again. I also gave up smoking cigarettes and felt the air around me become light and fresh. The last entry in my diary reads:

4 December 1996

Chez Lennon. Lennon on speed sketching Jen.

The Doors are on the hi-fi. I'm very stoned in a very purpose-ful, decisive, affirmative way. Perhaps the largest single change is that I feel at last relieved of my self-consciousness. Lennon knows and loves me. Even my dreams last night were all airy, light and relieved. Normal. I can feel that place in my mind again, that clear, empty chord just waiting to be played and rejoice.

I have felt quite ecstatic – but as I write this I am aware that I am still vulnerable, for some reason. There is some feeling of pain in me and I don't know what to call it.

Still, I am happy, and on the way up.

Part Two

Chapter Four

Tuesday morning, 9 December 1996 and it had been a typical weekend. Four of us had split a pill in Marc's car on Saturday night and gone to a couple of 'rad' clubs. First we had gone to look for Janine in Rush, one of Cape Town's newest and coolest house clubs. I had gone in still sober and alone while the others waited in the car, and woven my way through the masses of drugged bodies to no avail: she was not to be found. Next we had headed over to the G-Spot Lounge, a tiny but free club that played happy house. We quickly decided to leave and were getting into the car when Marc started coming on. He started dashing around on the pavement and then lay down unable to move, laughing hysterically. 'It was all good', as they say. We soon got him back in the car and made him drive us to Logos, our favourite club. The wilder the driving and the more it made me scream, the better. Logos was a trance-y, new-age place that consisted of one large warehouse-style room with dancing in the middle and chill-out cushions all around the walls.

By this time Marc was grooving along in between giggling about his moment of hysteria. We were all feeling more and more psyched up. In the lift the two buttons, up and down, and our selection of up, seemed symbols of our ascent to a higher state of bliss.

Up in the club, Lennon started to go off on a really 'rad' trip. He smiled beatifically at me. Elizabeth and I were still feeling sober. Happy but not tripping. To nudge it along I smoked a few drags of a good strong spliff.

The next thing I knew was that feeling from the desert again, but ten times more powerful. My teeth went rigid and my body and mind fell into a burning vortex beyond description. The overwhelming message from my body was 'Emergency! Poison! Emergency!' I gurgled to Lennon, 'I have to throw up.' Within seconds we were in the toilets and I had my finger down my throat desperately trying to get the pill out of me. I threw up again and again but the dreadful panic would not stop. The universe with me inside it was spinning out of control and my fear was abject.

As I threw up someone called in the girl from RaveSafe, an organization of young people trained to deal with drug emergencies who patrolled clubs and raves. They tended to be ravers themselves and I remember being strangely intimidated by her although she was perfectly pleasant. She kept saying, 'It's too late, the drug's already in her bloodstream. She's just going to have to wait it out.' I kept vomiting and panicking. Lennon was so drugged he could only lean against the wall smiling helplessly. He was so high he could barely realize something bad was happening. His uncontrollable smile pushed my terror through the roof.

After a length of time that could have been ten minutes or an hour, I had no more to throw up and started to seem back on the road to normality. The panic receded and we left the toilet and then the club. The others were all enjoying the effects of the drug, although they were, of course, concerned by what had happened to me. The four of us sat out on a wall on the street. They all thought I must have been unconsciously depressed and that the ecstasy had brought that to the surface. I was not so sure.

Then we were back in the car, speeding blithely along the quiet motorway to the forest. It was about 2 a.m. I was pretty sure I would never risk taking e again now the panic attacks were established as a pattern and the good effects so diluted. Still, I was feeling a mellow happiness by this time and was determined to make the most of the meagre high. We walked around the forest having conversations in a kind of heaven, talking about God and fairies and the nature of the universe. Then we drove home and crashed out just before dawn.

On Sunday and Monday we had all been coming down and felt a bit rough, but now it was well past the start of a new week and I felt back to normal. Lennon had to register as an undergraduate at the University of Cape Town that Tuesday so the two of us walked up there along the motorway. Suddenly it started, completely unexpectedly and without warning. A pain that was undeniable, yet had no physical pinpoint in my body. It was excruciating and unbearable. I felt as if I had been catapulted into another universe. Walking hurt, being outside hurt, but when we got to the university, being inside hurt too. Talking hurt. Nothing exactly hurt somatically, but rather waves of pain were radiating anxiously from my heart. I felt hot, tight and short of breath, as if I were having a panic attack that would not end. The only conclusion I could come to was that I was still coming down in some mysterious and horrible way.

But even resting later that day, back at Lennon's house, it would not go away. I lay as motionless as possible in the bright heat of the garden and inside in bed for two long days, able to stomach nothing more than a handful of raisins. I could barely muster the energy to speak. I did not know if it would ever end. That was the most frightening thing of all. I kept thinking that if it continued for a few more days I would have to kill myself: no-one could live with such anguish.

The house bustled with visitors and everyone around me was sympathetic, but no-one knew what was happening to me or what I was feeling. The others who had shared my pill were all feeling completely normal, so it appeared it was not a 'bad' e, unless all the badness had been concentrated in one quarter, which I had taken. Even if this had been the case, it still would not account for my history of bad reactions to other recent tablets.

People kept insisting that the pill must have brought out a latent depression. True, I had been down in previous months, but the week before taking the 'fatal' pill I had been in good spirits, and any down I had felt was itself linked to my ecstasy-taking. True, I had always been a 'worrier', one of those oversensitive people. I had spent most of my teenage years worrying that this or that person did not like me. Yet I had never known anything comparable to this. Throughout my life, I had experienced two kinds of low-level depression. One was a nauseous, heart-sore displacement when waking before dawn, going without sleep or coming down from drugs. The other was a textured, tangible, sinking feeling of grasping at thin air that occasionally held my consciousness for a split-second for no reason, too short a time to understand. I always thought it was a memory of a time before I could make sense of the world or use language, perhaps even of the trauma of being born. It is possible that these parts of my brain held the keys to a deep undiscovered anxiety and depression that ecstasy unlocked. If so, why did it happen with MDMA and not LSD or amphetamines? What I was experiencing now was not on the same scale as anything before – it was another pitch entirely, an unreal universe outside all previous experience. I thought it likely that any depression I naturally had within me would be switched on by this invading force, but that it was not the cause in itself. There was nothing in these two naturally dark spots in my brain that was a reason for this turmoil. They were mere sensations. The depression and anxiety I was experiencing were alien. Could this really have been lurking undiscovered within me all my life? Perhaps I was always destined to lose myself at eighteen? I found it impossible to convince myself that this horror was a dredged-up problem from my past: its character was palpably chemical, like being invaded by another being.

Later, I could rationalize it in terms of brain chemistry and a lack of serotonin, all fired out by the ecstasy, to which I must have been peculiarly sensitive, but at the time my mind pictured the experience cosmically. It was a black hole, a nothingness outside the world I had previously known and where no-one else could ever reach. No explanation convinced me, even a chemical one – it all felt much too psychological; too cleverly and precisely tailored to my own deepest private horrors. I felt in the presence of the devil, for real this time. I feared I had lost my soul, discovered a hell no-one else around me knew existed. The lack of serotonin made all previously good things hollow and ugly to me. It was like inhabiting a horror film. The glittering sea and sky of the Cape took on a threatening aspect. Friends showing me love were monsters in masks. I went down spirals into the black hole in my mind. All to a backdrop of total aloneness.

Elizabeth, a depressive herself, was able to understand that pain in the heart, ripping through the soul. On the second evening after it started, I sat in her house describing the pinpoint location of the problem, in my core, yet not quite physical. I was still not sure if this shockingly tangible sensation was depression or if it was some other mysterious illness. Pale and strong, Elizabeth confirmed she knew that pain in the heart, and that it was depression. Lennon, Marc and Lizle had all experienced some form of depression also. Lizle had stopped taking all drugs six months before, and she could now tolerate only gentle hobbies, like knitting, health-foods, folk music and aromatherapy. She had grown inexplicably old in her tastes, and, only now, I understood why. Yet none of them could see just how bad my suffering was behind my dulled exterior, and none of them recognized my pain as similar to their own.

Positive was now negative. I was afraid of happiness. The reason for this curious perception came back to ecstasy. Its highs and lows, during my first euphoric trip and this depression, were freakishly identical in content and structure. The e world worshipped certain values as godly: love, childhood, grinning, breathing deeply, nature, plastic, grace, excitement, heat, sparkly bright colours, the pleasure of saying 'I am happy'. Those 'godly' values were stamped forever on my mind in my first few experiences with ecstasy. Yet depression saw those values in a different light. I had no chemical capacity to process pleasure. All positive emotion was filtered through a pain so bad I retched with fear of it.

I became obsessed by my new terror of happiness. Everything I had loved, I now had to forgo, because it had turned to panic. A life's memories of a happy childhood, of rediscovering that joy on ecstasy, were now reassigned the mental label, 'fear'. My fear of happiness and love (in fact a fear of misery and panic, which I thought were happiness and love) bled easily across everything in life. Nature looked unspeakably ugly, particularly so for having previously been something I trusted. Nothing frightened me more than the extreme bliss brought on by ecstasy, which had done this to me. 'God is love,' proclaimed the signs outside churches, tearing holes in my fragile mind. Ecstasy was the love drug. Everyone knew that, including me. So ecstasy, the worst pleasure, the worst pain of all, was God. How could I fear love and God? I was surely the only person in the world to do so. It was a dangerous misapprehension. It was so true to me that I had panic attacks thinking I was happy or after saying the words 'I love you'. Now, I had to turn and run from all happiness.

I was balancing on a line of neutrality so fine it barely existed. I feared everything, most of all feeling happy. I lay in bed and wished I could cease all consciousness.

After two days of this, I felt I had no choice but to call my parents and ashamedly tell them what was happening. They had emigrated from Cape Town to Oxford in the 1960s to become academics. Now they were spending a Christmas holiday at Gran's house, and had no idea of my experimentation with drugs. They hardly even drank alcohol, let alone approved of anything more. Yet they took the news surprisingly calmly and with characteristic kindness. They came and fetched me, putting me to bed at Gran's with a bland, home-cooked meal. Sleep was my only respite from what felt like never-ending panic, so I tried to stay in its dreamland as long as I could every night.

The next day I smoked a cigarette and somehow the edge of the agony went. I wondered if all the awfulness was the effect of quitting smoking, as I had done three weeks before. Rationally I knew this was nonsense, but the association of not smoking with panic was one that prevented me quitting again for several years. After smoking I still felt almost unbearably bad, but no longer had my heart stretched open in permanent panic, there was 'just' anxiety with intermittent panic attacks.

My parents were going to Onrus, a charming seaside hamlet near the popular resort Hermanus, just a few hours' drive away, and suggested I go with them.

I lay on the back seat of the car. An hour into the drive, we stopped at a farm stall. It sold homemade fudge, jams, Boerewors, and baskets of guavas, melons and grapes. My mother and I sat on a seesaw in its gardens. On the horizon, elephant-like mountains stood, immovable.

'Does this cheer you at all?' my mother asked. 'Don't you think this heavenly?'

I stared blankly at the scene, unable to see what she saw. It was all covered in a suffocating film of unreality.

When we arrived in Onrus, Lennon and Elizabeth came out to visit. The four days we spent in a lovely whitewashed cottage were torture, since the problem was not improving. I did not know if I was depressed. All I knew was that consciousness was a nightmare. The clean, minimalist, all-white walls and furniture of the cottage magnified and reflected all fear. There was no messy corner to hide in. Outside was one of the most postcard-perfect lagoon beaches anyone could desire, one that dazzled its visitors with glistening sea and sand under cerulean African skies. All I could do was shudder at what appeared to me plastic scenery. I repeatedly tried little experiments to try to find a miracle cure. Swimming in the ocean should have taken my mind off my fear, but this was the kind of depression in which the mind is unable to forget the pain even for a second and I waded out comfortless. Orgasms were meaningless, pleasure-less twitches of muscle. I had lost all appetite for food and found I had dropped a stone in weight. My bleak new outlook was severe for everyone. They had to deal non-stop with my clinging and dependency.

We all returned to Cape Town frustrated. Two of my school friends from Oxford, Grace and Mitsuko, were due to arrive to stay with me for their holidays, Mitsuko for two weeks over Christmas, and Grace for a month or two. It had been planned for six months, and I was extremely concerned that I recover by the time we met. Unfortunately, when first Mitsuko and then Grace arrived during the weeks that followed, I was still utterly distraught, and they found I was not the same out-going, fun-loving person they had once known. Grace was more obsessed with make-up and looking smarter than ever. When the moment came to introduce her to Marc, I winced. He was wearing his tie-dyed patchwork trousers. I saw Grace's eyebrows ascend in disbelief. She reached for her Chanel make-up bag and retreated to the bathroom. She was equally fazed by Lennon's hair, and had to control her laughter when I introduced them. I felt sorry for her, surmised that someone like her could never understand my spiritual journey. Although our sisterly affection for each other remained, it was clear that we now had little in common. She had other friends in Cape Town, and she went to stay with them.

Mitsuko, who was staying with me and was dependent on me for entertainment, endured a disappointing holiday. Much of her two-week break was spent comforting me and taking me to see doctors. I forgot her birthday, which fell at the end of December, and she went into town alone where her bag was snatched. I was so lost I barely noticed. I tried to explain to both my old friends how, just a few weeks earlier, my soul had been killed, but they came from the 'straight world' and could not quite understand my tale of drug highs and lows. They saw the new me as a girl who was unbelievably dependent on her boyfriend to the extent she literally hid behind him and could not do anything without him. A strangely quiet girl who did not want to go out or have a good time.

I stayed with Lennon in his shared student house. He was faultlessly generous and caring, always by my side. We tried to take Grace and Mitsuko out, and there was a procession of long days and nights during which I sat mute and immobile trying to think my way out of the tortured cell of my mind while people danced, ate and drank around me. Every morning I woke unable to believe what had happened to me. My past self seemed to have been wiped out irretrievably. One typical afternoon I roused myself to go into the little shaded garden where Lennon, Marc, Mitsuko and Elizabeth were sitting playing guitar and smoking dope. They formed an idyllic scene in the golden sunlight. I accepted a few drags of the joint and moved to sit down under a tree. Its branches swept across my face. My heart suddenly lurched in panic. It started to speed up, rushing, rushing. I was soaked in a cold sweat, crying. Lennon helped me indoors. These panic attacks sprang up not only from smoking joints, which I soon learnt not to do anymore, but at any time, for no reason.

The depression was physiological. For the first few days I had thought it was a physical ailment, so forceful was the panic in my heart. Yet I realized instinctively that I had actually entered another realm of sensation, some no-man's-land between the physical and the mental. I seemed to be enclosed within a film of pain that I felt in my heart and my head and saw all around me yet which also seemed to be in its own bubble outside the universe. My way of breathing changed. For the first time in my life, I could no longer sleep unless the window was open. My short-breathedness and claustrophobia while panicking were recalled by any airless space. I was afraid also of breathing too deeply, since that was what people did on ecstasy, which reminded me of my panic attacks when rushing on e. This was unfortunate, since all the anti-anxiety self-help books I found recommended deep breathing. What would cure anyone else from depression was the one thing that would make me worse. It seemed that the relaxation of deep breathing could go too far and turn to panic. What was peace if too much of it became frightening?

A succession of magicians and doctors were consulted. First of all, a friend of Lennon's gave me a detoxifying green herbal drink made of barley three times a day. It tasted foul and changed nothing. Next, I saw a GP who was also qualified in alternative health. The one thing of which I was sure was that I needed someone who was open-minded enough to try to understand the cosmic horror of the experience, the fact that I feared for my very soul. Someone who would not take one look at me and prescribe tranquillizers and Prozac: ecstasy having reduced me to this, the very idea of taking another 'happy pill' made me panic. I was praying this doctor would miraculously understand what was happening to me as no-one else so far had. Elizabeth escorted me. In the waiting room, I was ready to rip my hair out with anxiety. Everything I saw, from the peaceful dried feinbos arrangements to the cosy wooden panelling on the walls, was turned sickening by the vapid monster in my heart. I could feel it in my heart, had identified it as undeniably, topographically there. It was nothing you could call a physical pain; the problem was clearly mental illness, yet it was causing a buzzing in my heart. It felt as if my heart had been opened and everything in the world was getting in, leaving me poisoned. The doctor was nonplussed but sympathetic and prescribed me Bach flower remedies and homeopathic pilules. I took them exactly as I was told over the three months that followed, but felt no dramatic improvement. They may have been a reason why my symptoms gradually eased over time, but I needed a wonder-cure, the answer.

The local drug advice centre offered a walk-in clinic, so Lennon and Mitsuko took me there. It was yet another day with the chemical, bizarre feeling of despair that wrenched the future away. A week of no change had turned into two and then three weeks, and my hopes for a cure were disintegrating. All I could see ahead was a lifetime of this. Surely the drug clinic must have some experience of such breakdowns? We sat in a room with two other drop-ins and were invited by the care worker to describe our problems. The other two, both middle-aged women who lived on the streets, were addicted to crack. After nodding to their stories, I briefly told the group what was happening to me, but it did not register with anyone. Drugs were a synonym for addiction as far as this clinic was concerned. The assistant kept warning me I had to stop taking ecstasy. I tried to explain that the thought of taking not just ecstasy, but any drug again, was as appealing to me as asking for another panic attack, and that therefore an addiction to ecstasy was the least of my concerns. It cut no ice however, and I was told there was little more to be said and packed off to the resident Reiki master. She promised me she would make my anxiety disappear but I felt nothing as she passed her hands over me, nor afterwards.

'Feeling all better now?' she asked as I got off the table.

'Um, yes, thank you so much.' I did not want to hurt her feelings.

The next choice could only have been psychiatry. My mother took me to the psychiatry department of the Groote Schuur Hospital one day. It was, unsurprisingly, a depressing place in itself. As I waited to be seen in a long grey corridor plastered with 'Suicide Is Not The Answer' posters, I pretended I was there to visit a sick relative. Half an hour later, I was assessed by an indifferent middle-aged doctor. Pleasingly unperturbed by my tale of woe, he told me that clinical depression usually lasts for six months and that I should therefore be feeling better in five months. I could not believe him, could not believe I could ever return to the normal world after what I had thought and felt those last few weeks. Besides, I did not think I could last for five more months. He offered me anti-depressants, but I was too wary to take any more happy pills.

Next I went to meet a medical school friend of my father's, a local professor of pharmacology. He noted down my case history for the records of any other scientists who chose to research the adverse psychological effects of ecstasy, and was gentle and thoughtful. But he had no answers. Then, after another session with a different, emotionless psychiatrist who recommended Valium, I decided to try psychotherapy. Lennon asked his Jungian therapist if he could recommend anyone for me to see, and I began going twice a week to Christina, an analyst in the leafy suburb of Claremont. I quickly apprehended what all initiates to Jungian analysis soon discover, that there is no advice or solution on offer. I kept asking Christina what I should do, what was wrong with my brain, only of course to be met with silence, 'Why do you ask that?' or a question about my dream the night before.

I wished only for a solution, but grew to appreciate the boundary Christina seemed to be able to draw around us. Her consulting room was the only place I felt safe from panic attacks.

Mitsuko returned to Oxford in early January. Before Grace's arrival, I had arranged for us to rent a studio in the seaside suburb of Muizenberg for a month. Muizenberg had always been my favourite beach, the location for countless morning swims with my family. On the Indian Ocean coast, the water was warm, and the sand stretched for miles. Muizenberg was a windy beach after ten o'clock, I discovered when we moved there. I was too apathetic to rouse myself early in the morning, so I barely spent any time there. Grace was disappointed with my choice of location for a holiday cottage. I had not realized she did not like sea swimming and would have preferred the fashionable, cold-water beach at Camps Bay. Muizenberg was a forty-five minute train or car journey from the city and trendy Atlantic shore. She felt isolated – my lugubrious state did not make for a fun atmosphere – and made plans to move into a youth hostel at the end of the month, while I would return to rent a room near Lennon in Observatory.

Halfway through January, my appetite returned. Marc and I went to a feast at a Hare Krishna temple one day and learnt to chant. Afterwards we went to a drumming café, a regular destination of ours in Observatory, and kept chanting. Soon everyone in the cafe was chanting with us. Grace, passing in the Porsche of her friend Adam, went in to see if we were there. She walked in to a vision of a roomful of hippies pounding drums and singing:

> 'Hare krishna
> Hare krishna
> Krishna krishna
> Hare hare
> Hare rama
> Hare rama
> Rama rama
> Hare hare'

It was too much for her. Her dry sense of humour had carried her through Marc's patchwork flares, Lennon's hair, our weird friends like Ann 'n' Jen, and my lifelong dottiness, but with this scene, it had met its match. She gazed at us for a moment, then turned and fled back to the Porsche.

I could laugh at such times, but then I would feel panic rising in me, and I would have to retreat to a silent corner to think. My dreams at night were of death. Gangsters would attack, rob and kill me, or I would be back at school, wandering friendless, a social outcast. One vivid dream concerned Anita Atkins, a member of the Cumnor Lot. She had been the dumpiest, most unpopular girl in the class. Now I dreamed *I* was Anita Atkins, and at the same time I was one of a group of murderers who had killed Anita Atkins 'because of e'. Murdering her was actually suicide. After the murder, her body lay in our house. We kept planning to take her out into the garden and bury her, but never did. I began to regret the murder and wonder why I had done it. The nation was in shock at this brutal murder. A psychic got through to Anita and she said, 'I am temporarily present.' Everyone was relieved, realizing that she had lived on after death. One of my murderous colleagues and I walked home together. I began to feel afraid of this friend who killed Anita with me. I remembered that it was she who had actually killed Anita, not me, and felt less guilty. I saw a magazine I had read a long time before I became a murderer (from August 1996), and could not understand how I had become a killer. I kept telling my friend we had to bury Anita, but she would not let me for the time being. I did not know who my friend was. She took on different faces, as if her identity was unknown. My analyst Christina had a field day with this dream.

Traditionally, it has been held across cultures and religions that to attain enlightenment or reach paradise one first has to suffer the dark night of the soul. True happiness can only be felt once the pilgrim has expunged all negativity through passion. Ecstasy opens up a new philosophical sensibility. With ecstasy, one is initiated into visionary heaven instantly, with no effort: in fact the experience comes as an unbelievable surprise. The first-time ecstasy taker suddenly realizes that love is the answer. It is an emphatically religious message that transforms and elevates most users' lives.

Yet there is no age-old story line to tell us what happens next. When paradise comes in the first chapter, the pilgrim has everything to lose instead of gain. You try to rediscover that state of consciousness by taking another pill and find that you can not quite get there. Almost there, so close that you decide it is just not as good a pill and if you can only find another pill like the first you took, maybe you could feel it again. Or maybe you were not in quite the right frame of mind the second time. So you keep taking more and more pills in larger doses, but that ecstatic, perfect feeling keeps becoming more of a hypnotic memory. You wistfully wonder if, having discovered heaven straight away, it is actually possible, in the grand cosmic sense of possible, ever to know it again.

For me this common ecstasy story was stretched to its most extreme tangent. My depression took the form of corrupted perfection. The awful perceptions with which it filled me were uniformly pictures of things that were supposed to be good but that through my eyes alone were gruesomely horrible. Everywhere I looked there were these good/bad things. Children, books about love, churches, paintings, happy song lyrics, words like 'I love you'. As well as running from bad, I felt I was running from good. Ironically, it was only now I realized how filled the world was with good things. It was almost impossible to escape from goodness. Of course I was equally afraid of badness – hatred, pain, cruelty and so on. I had to tread an impossible tightrope between the two. I was caught in an uncharted moral paradigm of ecstasy and its inverse emotions.

For years I had been, like most adolescents, swamped by insecurity. My worst fear had always been that no-one really loved me, or that they would not if they really knew me. Now I walked the streets and all I could see were people just as I had been. It became clear that it is, in fact, normal to be insecure. All everyone craved and needed was love.

I should have been enlightened and happy to have this vision and this power to reassure everyone that they really were loveable. Yet I now found I had a worse problem in the place of the old one. Normal people had social insecurities that were easy to solve – you just had to show them how loveable they were. I had a problem no-one else could cure. The problem was I was running away from love. In fact I was terrified of love, so terrified that my body would prickle and my heart race at the very mention of the word.

My very awareness of heaven had ruined its existence as far as I was concerned. I was living this out, this *Paradise Lost* tale of the bitter knowledge of good. I was a person who was going to think about the paradise I had been shown, who could not help questioning it. This analysis, this depressive doubt that seemed to have grabbed me without any sane, gentle beginning, forced me against my will to see evil in goodness. This led me to decide that pleasure and happiness and goodness and heaven were barred to me, as they were to Adam and Eve. It was the only story that reflected what was happening to me, and it was a story that seemed to alienate me from the rest of the human race. Adam and Eve had known Eden, and had then been condemned to suffer, and their children's children to suffer. Those children's children, the human race, my peers and I, were born ignorant of paradise, knowing it might exist but also told by all mystical tradition it was impossible to attain without the requisite suffering. It seemed to me that I had seen paradise through ecstasy even more than most people I knew. Of all my acquaintances, the smallest doses had made the most enormous impression on me. Humans were not supposed to feel what I had felt. Now, like Adam and Eve, I was cast from that garden of wonder into endless punishment for that knowledge I had taken for granted. While lucky, ordinary people suffered their whole lives through, retaining, by having never been truly happy, the ability to reach heaven, I was corrupted by knowledge of happiness and the way to paradise was thus forever barred to my soul. It was a complete reversal. I was jealous of anyone with worldly worries since they could still know that perfection was a dream they might find one day, in life or after death. Meanwhile I was graced with an unshakeable vision of a world crammed with love and goodness and the reality of heaven, all knowledge of which I truly feared, condemned me to eternal damnation.

As an ecstasy casualty, I was tormented by the new ground I had discovered. Where were the books, where was the wisdom about one who had already been to heaven? Only *Paradise Lost*, picked up from Gran's shelves, drawn in by its title, made sense.

'The mind is its own place, and in itself
Can make a Heaven of Hell, a Hell of Heaven.'

This dark night of the soul was not a prelude to paradise – it came after it. I sympathized entirely with Adam's words in *Paradise Lost* when he says after the fall from grace:

> 'How shall I behold the face
> Henceforth of God or angel, erst with joy
> And rapture so oft beheld? Those heavenly shapes
> Will dazzle now this earthly, with their blaze
> Insufferably bright . . . Cover me, ye pines,
> Ye cedars, with innumerable boughs
> Hide me, where I may never see them more.'

Opening a book about the polarity of good and evil, I skimmed over tales of Christian mythology in search of a solution to my problem. There was nothing, no answer, not even anything to grip me, which, I felt, was a pity, since the book had looked promising the day before. *Why Bad Things Happen to Good People* was also a washout, to my disappointment. Humans. People in society. Humanity seemed so conformist and inhumane in its striving towards God. Lennon's books, which included an interesting selection from the 1960s and 1970s, yielded some fragments. R. D. Laing gave me hope with the story of Mary Barnes, the psychotic (and even madder than me) artist he allowed to accept and live out her lunacy, resulting in a cure.

Meanwhile, life went on for everyone around me. My parents tried to persuade me to accompany them when they went home to England, but I was too afraid to leave Lennon, with whom I moved in temporarily. I had hardly seen my family, spending all my time as I did with Lennon, his family and his friends. Lennon started his first year studying fine art at the University of Cape Town. Meanwhile, Grace was having the best holiday of her life, leaving her teenage insecurities in the past as she discovered her free adult self. She wanted to go out all night, while I wilted at the thought of socializing. She was making dozens of friends, and allowing her soft inner character to emerge. She began to listen to African music. Casting inhibition to the wind, she sunbathed topless on the patio at her new backpackers' lodge. She became a relaxed person. She started to like Lennon and Marc after all.

In early January a group of us – Marc, Elizabeth, Lennon, his older cousins and myself – went cherry picking at a farm about three hours inland. I drove with the young folk. The route paralleled a long train of mountains and blazing, delicate veldt. It was the peak of a particularly hot summer, yet as always in the Cape, there was a playful breeze, and a mellow feel for such a grand sky.

We lit a spliff as soon as we were on the road, as always. I was hoping it would catapult me past the thoughts brooding and roosting in my head. As the drug's meditative profundity filtered through my mind, I felt a renewed uplift. I was indeed in a clear place, transcendent of depression. On the back seat of the car, in between Elizabeth and I, was a 1970s edition of the game Mastermind. We had owned the same edition at home in Oxford when I was a small child. On the box is a picture of a white-haired, bearded but glamorous man poised in a leather executive chair like a wealthy dabbler in the stock markets. A beautiful Asian young woman stands next to him, dressed to the nines in a cocktail gown. The room in which they are pictured is dark and mysterious in that way the 1970s, unlike the 1980s onwards, was not too cynical to advertise. The photograph reminded me of my perception of the world as a small child, when I had last seen it. 'Isn't it amazing,' I thought nostalgically. 'Wasn't my childhood perfect?' It was a rhetorical question. Yet no. Something about the woman in the picture suddenly looked submissive to me. Why was she standing up? Was she supposed to be the man's servant? It was a sexist picture, I realized – fine, forget it. But this – this means my childhood perception was flawed. I saw beauty as a child in a superficial, false picture that excludes and offends me. How could this be? Everyone knows the mind of an infant sees life in the most loving manner. It all came back to ecstasy, quick as a flash. On ecstasy I had felt like a child – had even, in that best moment, relived my childhood. In heaven, on ecstasy, when we are at our best, we see the world through the eyes of a child. Of course we make mistakes in that trust as children, burning ourselves on stoves and doing whatever strangers tell us to do because we know no evil. An adult can not become a child again because an adult can never recapture that innocence. Yet it is the best way to be, the way of the fool. But I kept thinking that this was wrong. It was not practical or good to be so trusting as an adult on ecstasy, who sees the world like a child and believes everything is good. There is evil in the universe and everyone tries to cover it up but it exists, I thought. I had recently found solace in William James' conclusion in *On The Varieties of Religious Experience* that 'it may be that there are forms of evil so extreme as to enter into no good system whatsoever'. Solace because, having read James' catalogue of religious melancholia, I could see I was not the only person to become so morbidly obsessed with the problem of evil as to find 'healthy-mindedness pure and simple . . . unspeakably blind and shallow'. Yet, alone in it or not, the problem of evil remained.

Violently, I saw myself fall down a spiral. It almost had the force of hallucination. I was dumbstruck, slipping into a black hole. I felt a paralysis creep indomitably over me like rigor mortis. I was dying of fear and I could not speak. The mountain sped by and it was laughing at me. Its lines looked like mocking faces in the epic, godlike rock. The cruelty of nature stung, and I could not bear to look closely. Yet it was all around, inescapable. In panic, I leant forward, shocked at myself, and cried out to Marc, who was driving, 'Please, can we stop the car? I need to stop. I need to get out. I'm panicking.'

He hesitated, loath to indulge my overreaction.

'I need help,' I staggered out, the words like a foreign language. 'Seriously, I need help. Please.'

'Olivia, do you really need to stop?' said Lennon.

'You promised,' I said. 'You said if I feel bad you will help.'

So we pulled over. The panic attack faded quickly as it usually did, though every time I had one I thought it was the end. After a half hour straying along the road on foot and sitting on the grass beside it, we got back in the car and drove to the farm.

The fearful thing about the imagery of depression is simply that one can not understand why one's own mind conjures up such terrifying evil. There is no reason for it, nothing real in the world so awful as the mind's phantasmagoria of monsters. There is typically nothing ugly in the character or desires of a depressed person apart from their fearful imagination. Anxiety is often mere fear of fear. Yet if one lives in fear of more formless fears, they can become as real as any other belief. It is dangerous, striking out into the depths of the imagination, tampering with accepted constructs of love and happiness. Beliefs become traps and it is possible to lose sight of the natural laws of reality that keep one sane. Being close to the edge, I kept faltering, like a vertiginous mountain-climber clinging to the side of a peak, who feels the earth, thousands of feet below, inexorably pulling.

This is why one of the most alienating atmospheres of depression is of inhabiting an unreal space outside the world. I saw myself on a rock of darkness deep in space, far from the enclosed sphere of reality experienced by all around me. Everything in the unreal universe was an all too precise inversion of real life. Good was bad, truth was a lie, beauty was ugliness and pleasure was pain. These things constantly obstructed all normality of consciousness. During all my eighteen years I had never felt a glimmer of this sensation of unreality. I asked everyone, 'Have you ever felt like you were not real? I mean, that you are in an unreal space?' I hoped someone might say they knew what I meant and explain it all to me as part of existence. This would have given it a boundary. Sure enough, some people said they kind of understood, and then I would press them on the details and unbelievable pain of it and it would emerge that they meant something normal, were referring to simple existential angst.

Even on the good trips, ecstasy had sometimes made me see things in a way that made me deeply uneasy: plastic, robotic, tooth-grinding perspectives. People became automatons when they were high; their emotions were automatic chemical reactions staged by the drug. I found it hard to believe that love could be reduced to chemistry alone, but ecstasy showed that humans really were just puppets with a master chemist pulling the strings. I was haunted by the memory of Lennon in the toilet at Logos as I vomited up my e, the stupid grin twitching on his face uncontrollably. Happiness was not a choice in e-land – it was a compulsion. Now I understood the imagery of Cupid's arrow: you did not choose to love, love made you love.

The drug was the reflection of society with its corporate, branded encouragement of not thinking. Raves were sponsored by this exploitative trainer company or that unhealthy soft drink. Ravers were so happy to buy anything. Ecstasy said be happy, be stupid, be fake. Hear your e-induced voice saying, 'I am happy.' Question that? You're not really happy? It doesn't matter. Be stupid. It was so far from any other drug and drug philosophy. The antithesis of a drug like LSD that drenches the taker's vision in acidic truth. Quite different from the culture of opiates, which involves both sordid injections and thoughtful heavens. Ecstasy was clean and mindless, like plastic. As for speed, it was not a psychological drug, it did not promise to lift you onto another plane. Cocaine people were commonly held to be egotistical and arrogant, a world away from the purring virtue of e-people. Those drugs were passé. E was the prom-queen of drugs: Miss Popularity herself. If you wanted to take acid, you were a dork. Heroin, you were a loser. Coke, you were stuck in the 1980s. You were cool and hardcore by mixing these drugs with e, but without e they were suspect.

E is grace. Grace is religious. God-given, smooth beauty. Grace is the posture, the walk, the dance, the perfection of speech on ecstasy.

The sense of reward from on high. Standing up tall like a Greek god. Do you really feel pure when you feel grace? Isn't there an element of falseness in it, of posing, of glossing over hard rough reality? God give you grace. Amen. Turn from grace? Turn from God. I don't want to be bad. But I can't stop being afraid of grace. That heaven is too much. How can anyone call their child Grace? How can anyone not be afraid? Am I the only person to fear God?

Chapter Five

January and February ticked by and I moved into a room in a house on Ivy Street, under the bridge that links downtrodden Mowbray with boho Observatory. The family I lodged with were your average hippie Obs people. Suzie, a plump reflexologist with long curly blonde hair, her husband River, a shaggy-haired dopey guy with John Lennon glasses, their cute little boy Fred and a couple of dogs, Stanley and Brewster. I hid away from them, telling them nothing of my devilish outlook on life, and they must have taken me for an unfriendly, stuck-up kind of girl who rather than deigning to speak to them simply borrowed their Shirley MacLaine books and forgot to return them. These quasi-spiritual books, supplemented by a diet of back issues of *Odyssey*, the local eco-friendly magazine, afforded me little enlightenment; however they were all I could find, once sequestered in that little house.

Obs was a world of people who not only believed in fairies and angels but wore tie-dyed t-shirts depicting the little 'love-miracles'. It was a world where you might find a grey-haired man of a distinguished age pretending to be a lion outside the Spar supermarket: 'I am a lion! Rooooaaaaaaar!', rearing up on his 'hind' legs. These men were frequently surrounded by young girls who hung on their every word. The old men hung out in their tents at raves playing didgeridoos, flicking their long beards, were the ones handing out the tabs of acid and ecstasy, not to mention the 'candy flips' that were half ecstasy, half acid. Back on Lower Main Road, the centre of Obs, you might pass half a dozen beggars on every block. Most of them had been living on those streets for years and were tolerated and partially fed by the kind-hearted yuppie-hippie restaurateurs. Everyone knew everyone. The deeper you got into the 'scene', the more 'hectic' it became and the more like a 1960s California microcosm bizarrely lost in space and time at the bottom of Africa.

Every tourist falls in love with South Africa. I had loved it passionately all my young life, and now that I had lived there nine months, felt it was my home. My accent – which like that of some others always mimics that of wherever I go, not out of choice but in fact despite my efforts to retain my English bearings – had become South African: 'Howzit bru.'

'Cool, man.'

'Is it. Kif.'

I loved replying 'is it', relishing that contrary to all appearances it was not a question but a statement of agreement, like the English 'oh really?' but spoken without any hint of a question mark.

I had Christina, the analyst my parents paid for me to see twice a week, and the room in Ivy Street, also funded by my parents, since I was too depressed to find a job. I was a spoilt eighteen-year-old girl who didn't know anything on the outside, and on the inside I was a lone pawn in a terrifying battle between good and evil that no-one else seemed to grasp.

Every day I simply followed Lennon wherever he went. When he was at lectures, I stayed in his bed, crying. His dog, Nancy, would come to comfort me, placing a sympathetic paw on my hand and staring into my eyes. That would make me cry even more. I could no longer trust, not even this pure-hearted animal. I sat though films and dinner parties barely able to concentrate for the pain in my heart.

I felt I still had to admire good things, but that respect was not genuinely *felt*. All those supposedly good things seemed fake. Loving them, loving God, loving childhood innocence, loving heaven, loving a boyfriend, feeling any kind of love, I did not consciously allow. But I felt love's obligation – the eerie sense of being forced by the universe to love, even now when love was full of panic for me. Love that everyone else chose, had to force me, and I could not help but feel it was bad. Love was bad. These seemed taboo words and they mystified anyone to whom I blurted them.

If e is heaven, could I really be the only person who would not want to rush for all eternity, I wondered. It did not enter my mind that e was not heaven. Ever since my first wonderful ecstasy experience, my emotions had been viewed through ecstasy's prism. I could no longer differentiate between my childhood and the way ecstasy makes you feel like a child. Or between my spontaneous un-drugged emotion, *I love this*, and that identical emotion forced into being by ecstasy, sometimes excitingly, sometimes crudely and falsely. The emotions were in many cases identical, chemical reactions in my brain.

I was unable to realize in this state that ecstasy was not really godly and infallibly good and had not taken me to heaven. It took two years to free myself from this absurd but very common belief. In time, I would be able to see that while I had often been happy on ecstasy, that did not make ecstasy definitive happiness, and that many aspects of its high, most notably the stupidity and love of plastic people experience, are of course neither virtuous nor godly nor pleasant, at least to me. But at this time, I was locked in the belief that the ecstasy experience was contact with definitive happiness.

That scorching summer I lay in the breeze of a fan, reading everything available in the search for a tale of someone afraid of happiness. There was nothing, but William Styron's *Darkness Visible* came closest to describing the harrowing 'interior doom' sensation of anxiety. It was a relief to read of a nightmare like mine (though I did not allow myself to feel it, for I thought I was afraid of relief).

Grace returned home, a sun-kissed, mellow party-goddess. I had been able to give her nothing, not even a smile or a friendly word on many days. Olivia was no longer the exuberant person she once knew. I couldn't care anymore if people liked me or how I looked. It should have been liberating: the less effort I made, the more people seemed drawn. But I no longer wanted love. The more I ran from it, the more people wanted to make friends. It was a nightmare. People kept saying I had never looked better. It was beyond me to understand this. I posed for photographs, sure that the agony inside would be visible, that the light I felt missing from my soul would make me appear grey. But when the photos came out I looked tanned, slim and healthy. My false, razor sharp smiles appeared as gentle happiness. Although I was surrounded by friends, all closeness that could not help me survive I let wither and die. I had no energy to keep frivolous relationships alive. Lennon, Lizle, Cara, Elizabeth and Marc stood by me like a family – I demanded nothing less of them – but my other friends were nonplussed by my moroseness, and we grew apart. I was no longer available to go out with, to take drugs with, even just to share a joke. My newer friendships with Alice, Mandy and Ann 'n' Jen became silent tundras of non-conversation. My letters to my old schoolmates back home halted.

By March, the panic attacks had lessened in frequency. I had not had one for several weeks. I dared to hope (without feeling the hope) that I might be recovering. Then one day catastrophe struck. I had spent the afternoon at Marc's, writing a short story on his computer, a darkly comic story about the different forms of counsel offered in response to a single problem – based, of course, on my own recent therapeutic experiences. As I finished the story I had a feeling of setting all my powers free, giving the ending everything I had, and I felt for once I had done something constructive. I closed the document, the computer crashed, and the story vanished. Marc came to help me, but the computer had not saved it. It was lost. A painful but small thing in the great pattern of life, but it turned an unconscious key.

I returned to the house on Ivy Street and lay down on my bed. A nervous panic was ebbing and flowing at the edge of my veins. I smoked a cigarette, trying to muffle it. Then I felt an indescribably awful thing. My eyes were closed and I felt myself in a kind of hallucination, falling down a long red bloody fleshy chute into hell. I was alone in a black hole, exiled out to the limits of space, alone forever in this endless agony. The vision lasted only a second, but the recognition of aloneness and doom was strong. It seemed proof to me of hell's existence within the mind, as a place where the mind could easily go and from which it might never return.

I could not kill myself in case I found myself in hell. The only way out of such a mental hell in life or death would be to wish or will yourself out of it, but since I was afraid of God, I could do no such thing.

The torment of this was too much. I am not sure what happened for the next few hours, since the whole evening was one I later blocked out of my mind, in a conscious effort to forget it. The next thing I remember is telephoning my parents at four in the morning in the UK and telling them I needed help. They suggested I fly straight home, but I couldn't wait that long. Deeply worried, they called my mother's cousin Bobby and asked him to come and fetch me to his house in Hout Bay. I waited for Bobby outside on the stoep, in my nightie, chain-smoking Winstons to slow my beating heart. He drew up in his car forty minutes later, helped me in and began asking me what was wrong as we drove along the deserted motorway. Bobby was a moody psychologist, who treated a dozen patients at a smart clinic in Camps Bay. When he was happy, there was no-one more engaging. My enduring memory of Bobby was of him slamming out songs by Jerry Lee Lewis, Phil Collins and other classic rock musicians on Gran's piano every Shabbat, bellowing the lyrics in his electric blue shirt to a captivated audience of old ladies and toddlers.

I answered all his questions fully, as always wishing for a miracle of 'oh, I know what to do'. But his outlook on me seemed bleak: 'It's not good,' he muttered.

At his house he tried to persuade me to take some tranquillizers. I refused in terror of being *made* to calm down, as e had
made me happy. The very sentence construction, 'made happy',
or the advice, 'calm down', reeked of force and conformism. I
was lost to happiness, out of the whole circle.

'You should take them – your case seems a psychotic one,'
Bobby said, 'and I will take you to see Leon Hendleman
tomorrow.'

'Who's he?' I asked.

'He's one of the greatest psychologists in Cape Town, an old
friend of mine. He can analyse you and do some tests. He's like
a bunny rabbit, you won't be afraid of him – he helps everyone
who sees him.'

It sounded hopeful, but I was too afraid to take the pills.

'But you need them, Olivia,' Bobby insisted. 'Come on
now, here's some water.'

It seemed like a scene from *Woman on the Edge of Time*. I
was terrified of pills. I didn't want to be happy or calm. I was
afraid of everything. Had he not heard anything I had said? I
must be coming across as too crazy to be understood.

The next afternoon I was taken to see the eminent psychologist in his office. He did indeed resemble a bunny rabbit,
plump, white-bearded and dopey.

'Hello, Olivia – why don't you sit down and tell me about
what happened last night?' he started.

I was terrified that I was psychotic, and still shaking from
my vision of falling lost and damned into an eternal black hole
the evening before. I tried to speak sanely and show myself
to be in control and intelligent. I told him everything, and
scrutinized his face for a hint of comprehension.

115

He looked kindly concerned, and reached for a clipboard. 'Now I would like to ask you some specific questions, to establish the type of your disorder. Ahem, we can start off with the schizophrenia characteristics. Now, do you or have you ever heard voices?'

'I don't have schizophrenia!' I said, horrified. 'And I am not psychotic, I am sure of it.'

'That's fine,' he replied all too calmly, 'I am sure you are quite right. Let's just use these tests as a way of establishing the angle of the problem. So have you been hearing voices – or seeing anything that wasn't there?'

'No – not really,' I answered. 'I mean, I kind of felt or saw something last night but it wasn't like I actually thought it was there – I mean I knew where I was, and it was more a feeling. Once or twice in the last year I have heard a voice saying my name, and it was coming from inside my head, it was my mother's voice, the voice she uses to call me. It didn't frighten me. That's all, I have never heard or seen anything else whatsoever.'

'Ahh. And do you ever feel a need to wash yourself or your surroundings more often than necessary?'

'No.'

'And who is the president?'

'Nelson Mandela.'

'And if you had to rate your level of depression today on a scale of one to ten where ten is the highest, how would you rate it?'

'Eight,' I said supplicatingly, wishing he would adjudge me sane, for I did not feel insane.

He asked a few more questions then pronounced, 'You have

116

scored highly for both borderline psychotic and personality disorders. Now I am going to suggest you start off trying some anti-depressants and tranquillizers, and then . . . well, we will see how things go. We must get you back to normal functionality before you start at university in October, eh? Of course, if you are not ready then, there are many options and places here for help. I am sure we will be able to try any one of a number of other possibilities . . . '

So it had come to this. I saw Valkenburg, Cape Town's notorious mental hospital, suddenly on the agenda. It was just down the road from me in Obs. Or would it be some nice little mental home in Oxfordshire? My middle-class education and eighteen years of grooming to be a mistress of the universe, even conceivably a psychologist myself, casually assuming I would always be on the side of power, suddenly inverted, erased and stamped insane. It was humiliating.

I did not believe him. I knew I was not mad enough for medication and incarceration yet.

'Are you sure those are the standard tests?' I dared to ask.

'I'm afraid so,' he said laughing.

'I don't want to take anything,' I said, explaining again that taking happy pills was one of my greatest fears.

'Well, take my prescription anyway – they'll not hurt you, I promise. They are quite different from ecstasy. It is your only hope to really lift you out of this mess, as I see it.'

Cousin Bobby was brought back in to hear the diagnosis and take the prescriptions. 'Good luck,' called Leon, waving us goodbye.

I had seldom felt so embarrassed and crazy. I knew I was not really insane, hallucinating giant pandas or hearing messages to set my home on fire. I believed in the wisdom of the fool, in the rights of the oppressed, I had read artists' indictments of psychology's insane judgements of insanity from Sylvia Plath to Shakespeare.

How were these pills supposed to help me when I could not even bring myself to touch the surface of the packet, for fear it would be like taking e again? Ever since the depression had started, I had been overwhelmingly wary of touching anything e-related. Anything an ecstasy-taker had touched, I would not touch. I was obsessive in my adherence to this principle, but it had a rational basis, a fear of making the depression worse by taking ecstasy again mistakenly.

I was driven to Gran's house in picturesque Sea Point. Bobby dropped me off with Gran and Shirley, her carer. Gran, who had always suffered from epilepsy, was losing her memory as a result of a lifetime on anti-fit medication. She still recognized most people most of the time, but her thoughts were jumbled and latched on to whatever seemed uppermost in her mind. This had often led my hippie friends to hang in her every word, acclaiming hers as an enlightened state of consciousness. She had a religious soul, not merely in the devout Bible-reading sense, but in an innate spirituality she possessed. I paced her house searching for something to unlock my aloneness, and found Gran's poems and papers and annotations on books. Some notes she had written perhaps forty years before on the horror of having an epileptic fit seemed relevant to my own dread.

It always struck me as particularly sad for Gran that Shirley, though plainly kind, was not herself an educated or spiritual person. She did not read what my family considered to be 'good' books – the classics. She preferred soap operas – to my clan, a heinous offence against culture. Every day she wore an identikit pyjama-like outfit, a shapeless sweatshirt and stretchy bottoms to cover her obese figure. Gran was essentially alone the majority of her days with only this boor with a crew-cut for company. So Gran was living the best she could, wandering ceaselessly through her silent halls, murmuring about poetry and her childhood, repeatedly searching for her hairbrush, while from behind Shirley's locked door came the canned sound of TV laughter.

I was shown, as always, to the nursery, the room in which my mother had slept as a child. I had heard her stories of finding a lizard on the ceiling, and I had once been locked in there by mistake. I picked up L. M. Montgomery's *Emily* series from Gran's bookshelves. I winced at its happiness, which I had once found entrancing. Here was the tale of a girl like me, who wanted to be a writer. As an innocent young lady in turn of the century Canada, she never had her psyche invaded by drugs. I felt bitterly envious of this storybook character.

In this house, I was unreachable. Neither Gran nor Shirley understood the depth of my panic, and I had no hope of making either understand. All I could think of was the moment of horror back in my rented room, the vision of myself falling into a black hole of doom. It seemed a prophecy.

Alone in the nursery, paralysed by the deadly collective insanity of the household, I stared at the anti-depressants, afraid to touch them. They looked so physically harmless. But the leaflet noted their effects on serotonin and dopamine. Like e, I thought. It would be like taking another e. I could not.

The next day was Shirley's day off. Gran was to be left alone with a temporary carer. Bobby asked Shirley to take me with her to her parents' house in the southern peninsula, and she kindly agreed. I stayed there for a night, just me in the dark guest room, a meal brought to me on a tray. I never met the family. Unable to sleep, I took a tranquillizer. It sent me into a slowed-down, groggy doze. I was relieved that my flagging energy seemed to have trumped the risk of panicking again – my mind had been whirring at such a pace it clearly could not have gone overboard, although the idea of swallowing a tranquillizer was frightening.

In the morning, Shirley drove back to Gran's with me at her side. Two hours later we were getting ready to drive to my Obs room to pick up some of my things. My mind was whirling. I went to sit out on the stoep, my feet on the lush emerald grass. I had nothing to lose, I supposed.

'We must go now, Olivia, we've got to get back for Gran's hair appointment at one,' called Shirley.

I went inside and before I could think, I held the tablet between my fingers – it's too late now, I've touched it – and put it in my mouth. Swallowed it down, done. Now just wait and see. I was being optimistic. It couldn't have any effect, I knew. Not until I had been taking the pills every day for weeks. I had nothing to fear. But really, I was petrified.

'Come on, let's get in the car.'

We got in. Shirley driving, Gran next to her, me in the back. Silence. We drove for several miles. The word 'petrified' was taking on a certain resonance. I sensed its truth. I might turn into stone. I was so scared I might go utterly mad. Go to that place, that hell. The terror was eating me up. Petrified, petrified, petrified. The world seemed to be closing in. Was this the pill I had just taken? Was I on e? I kept silent, hoping it would recede.

We reached Observatory and Shirley asked me for directions to my house. I gave them, but as I spoke the fear was competing for my attention. The more I tried to quell it, the higher it rose up. I'm on Serotonin, I thought. Gran was becoming agitated, asking questions. I became aware my heart was beating heavily and I realized the fear was swallowing me. The panic attack was like an orgasm in reverse. First the beating heart, then an exploding road to the end: in this case, madness. My body started to heat up and shake uncontrollably, and my fingers, then my hands, began to prickle. 'By the pricking of my thumbs, something evil this way comes.' Paralysis swept through my arms with the prickling. They would not move. My voice came out instinctively as never before, as a series of animal moans. I forced it into terrible sounding words: 'Help me . . . help me . . . take me to hospital . . . I'm dying.' There was not enough voice to say any more. I caught sight of my once-sane, now psychotic face in the rear-view mirror. My eyes reached out to myself calling, 'PAIN'.

Gran looked confused and frightened and I felt ashamed. But I had no control. I thought I was dying, poisoned by the 'e' I had just taken. I could not move my upper body, could hardly breathe. We were by now right outside my house.

'Is this it?' Shirley stopped the car. I managed to gasp 'Yes.'

She bundled me out onto the street, Gran flapping anxiously by our side. She had not realized there was anything wrong with me until now.

As soon as Shirley rang the doorbell the panic began to fade and I felt embarrassingly alive. What on earth was Suzie going to think when she opened the door? She had not even been expecting us.

'Oh! My God! What's wrong?' she exclaimed on seeing us thronged on her veranda. 'Olivia, are you all right?'

'Yes, sorry, sorry,' I replied. 'I . . . ' I could not explain.

'She just started screaming like something horrific,' blustered Shirley. 'We were just coming to fetch her things. This is Thelma Rhodes, her gran.'

'Oh my goodness, well. Come in, come in,' said Suzie, ushering us inside. Gran and Shirley were cloistered in the lounge while Suzie put me to bed in my room. I had never told her I had any problems before, but now, as she perched warily on the edge of my mattress on the floor, I told her everything. Now the panic was gone, I felt shame and relief, but still doom.

A reflexologist by trade, she worked on my feet for free, said ecstasy might have released my heart chakra, much like doing Kundalini yoga without adequate preparation. She was horrified by what she found as she palpated my feet. Apparently, my soul was wide open, overwhelmed by all the energy flooding in and out and at risk from anything negative.

'I can't believe you've been walking around in this state,' she cried compassionately. 'You must have been taking in so many bad vibes every time you walked down the street – I'm surprised you've coped.'

She advised me to imagine a barrier forming around my heart or a plug stopping the gap, but the sense of panic rushing through my heart was too powerful to respond to visualization.

'Gosh,' she said finally, 'if only we'd known what was going on with you. We just thought you were a moody bitch. If we'd known you were actually depressed, we'd have understood.'

So this was how my depression was making me appear on the outside. I was chastened. I remembered how over the last couple of months I had shut myself away in my room, mooched helplessly in the face of this kind family's smiles.

I wondered what Gran was thinking. I heard the front door close as Shirley led her back to the car for her hair appointment. I threw the pills away.

That evening, I saw Lennon. Ashamed of my ongoing catastrophes and wanting to allow him a break, I had not wanted him to know about this latest crisis. The panic attack outside my house was the worst I had experienced. I did not want to burden him, but when I finally did tell him the events of the last few days, he reassured me of my safety.

'If you die first, will you find me when I die and make sure I am brought to heaven? And if I die first, will you look for me as soon as you die and rescue me from hell or purgatory?' I asked him insistently. 'I might not be able to look for heaven myself – I might be too afraid. I need someone to take me there.'

'I promise,' he replied.

His housemates and I shared a cosy supper. They, like Lennon, took my fears not as psychosis, but as mere fears. They were outraged by my cousin's insistence that I was mad and that I needed tranquillizers. Their acceptance diluted the fear.

The next day I talked to Marc. He was about to set off on a trip to England, where he hoped to stay with my family, and then work and travel around Europe. I decided to return home with him for a month or two. It was now March – I had been away almost ten months. The idea of seeing my home again was emotive. I wondered how I would react to those familiar streets and rooms with my new horror of childhood nostalgia.

Chapter Six

The trip over was hellish. I had bought one of 1997's bestsellers, *Emotional Intelligence*, from a scanty selection at the airport, but I could not get past the Introduction. My brain was churning with worry: I had not been able to conquer the black-hole fear. My mind had not felt peace now for three months, except in sleep, which I did as much as possible. As soon as one problem was resolved, a new one took its place, and the fears I wrestled with, of eternal damnation from every possible angle, were so disabling that I could not carry on experiencing life until each and every one was solved. So I spent the twelve-hour flight worrying incessantly.

Marc was predictably charmed by Oxford, and we soon settled into our 'temping holiday'. Days were spent sightseeing or working as waiting staff. One day we cycled out to Blenheim and back along the river. After the bright, insistent exuberance of Africa, England's bare black and silver trees and muted fields were a relief to my mind, weighed down by fear of happiness. It was the first time I ever saw trees portraying emotion. Branches in postures cast by the wind made trees look wistful, lonely, frothily sociable. Once I had this anthropomorphic vision, it stayed. I was almost happy, and for periods of time that day, I found I could put my mental torment in a relatively safe place in the back of my mind, temporarily solved until later. When I was alone, it unravelled.

Yet the panic attacks did not resume. When Marc and I were listening to Neil Young and David Bowie and quietly chatting in Oxford pubs, I could sense that I was so ready for happiness that my decree that I was scared of joy became absurd. Even working together as contract waiting staff at Oxfordshire hotels and marketing fairs was almost pleasant.

Marc was my model friend. He was depressed, but he laughed at every little thing.

The only problem was worry. It plagued me whenever I was alone or without distraction. We went on long coach journeys around the country, visiting the Brontë house in Haworth and Arianne and Leila at university in Newcastle and Leeds. I spent those journeys locked in my mind's internal obstacle course, unable to appreciate anywhere we went. My brain had never worked so hard without rest. In later life I could not make myself analyse with the same stamina. This pinnacle of sharpness was driven by desperation.

When we were in Oxford, my childhood home fed me a diet of strange memories and perceptions. I read letters my sister had kept, from friends of hers congratulating her on her 'adorable' baby sister, sixteen years before. I wished I could start again as that perfect self. The living room, about which I had rapturously fantasized in my raver days as the epicentre of my infant memories, was now a sinister no-go area for me for the very same reason. Ecstasy culture's adulation of all things childlike now made me question whether I could trust my own happy memories of being young. Was this not also false happiness? Was not my childhood innocence and virtue false? My childhood now seemed dubious and disturbing. It was intensely painful to look at all the old things in the house and have to negate each one as a lie, as something to fear.

I was a lie. I was horror itself. Everything is lost to me now. My best self is lost. I am stuck in a memory of pain I can never deny, pain that stunts me at the supper table: 'What's wrong?'

'Fine,' staring away.

Pain that makes eighteen years vanish.

How could such a thing be possible?

I'm on the other side of the universe. Pain is something inconceivable when you're not experiencing it. Maybe that's why happiness feels inconceivable when pain strikes.

What I can't stand is that constant desire to feel better, that resilience, that positivity. It's always there.

I can't stand acknowledging this. It feels DANGEROUS, truly dangerous.

I hate all my desires. I hate the part of me that says 'make me feel better', all soft and gentle. It feels sinister, wheedling.

Maybe I'm possessed by evil to feel this hatred and fear of something the rest of the world idolizes and I used to idolize when I was pure.

This is ugly, not beautiful in any way.

I began to have nightmares about Gran. I would be in her house, approached by her in her long front hall. She would be calling me, 'I'm coming, I'm coming.' I would realize she was psychotic. I would try to shout, to run, but she was getting closer, right into my space, arms outstretched, 'What can you do? What can you do?' repeating from her mouth. In another dream, my mother, father, Cousin Bobby and I were seated at dinner with Gran, and, while the adults were talking obliviously, Gran leaned towards me and told me she was having horrific, terrifying hallucinations, again murmuring, 'What can you do? What can you do?' After dinner, she chased me like a zombie, and I called out 'Help' but no sound came. On waking, it always surprised me how textbook my horrors were.

I dreamed again of Anita Atkins. This time, I returned to school and found she was in fact alive, despite her murder. I apologized to her for killing her, and she forgave me.

I saw most of my old schoolmates again, one after the other, and without exception it was clear I had nothing in common with them now. We had nothing to say to each another. It was embarrassing. They would advance, greeting me sparklingly, and I would emerge as if from a ditch of sorrow, with no words, only a mountain of pain to ignore. At each farewell, both parties knew it was goodbye for the last time.

I went to see Dr Nathan, my GP. I had always found her manner matter-of-fact to the point of unfriendly, so I asked my mother to come with me for moral support. Within five minutes she was pressing me to take Prozac and tranquillizers. I declined. A friend of my mother's recommended a psychotherapist who had helped her daughter recover from depression. Dr Valerie Gough had a handsome office in a traditional rambling North Oxford house. She was a rather stiff, old-fashioned lady of sixty-five. I immediately liked her but realized she knew nothing of ecstasy. My problems were too modern and uncouth for her. I was grateful to see her two or three times, but I knew I still needed specific help.

My next stop was a local homeopath, a Dr Martin I found in the Yellow Pages. I cycled to his office through the serene North Oxford streets populated by bearded academics on bicycles, their baskets filled with baguettes and their stained tweed hems tucked into fluorescent cycle clips. Their cosy, eccentric intellectual air comforted me. When I entered Dr Martin's wood-panelled consulting room, I was pleased to see magazine clippings acclaiming his excellence in frames on the wall, along with numerous certificates and diplomas. When I had poured out my story, he was intrigued.

'I have never come across a case like this with ecstasy, I must say,' he admitted. 'I have seen one or two people whom I was able to help to stop taking the drug. But that's not really your trouble, is it?'

He looked at me with understanding in his eyes.

'No, exactly,' I replied. 'Taking ecstasy again is my greatest fear in this world. I need something to make me less afraid of happiness.'

'Hmm.' He thought for some time, and then said, 'I have had success treating people who have had similar problems after smoking cannabis. People who have had a bad experience after smoking it and need to somehow undo the damage. Of course, you know once you open this kind of door in the mind, you can not ever close it. But you can get over it, go on to live a normal life, master it and overcome whatever has traumatized you. Normally what I would do is prescribe you a fraction of whatever it is that has poisoned you. Of course I can't give you a homeopathic version of MDMA, but I can give you a fraction of THC, the active ingredient of cannabis. So maybe if we tried out a homeopathic treatment for cannabis poisoning on you it might have a chance. It's worth a try, anyway.'

'That makes complete sense to me,' I said. 'I haven't been able to smoke cannabis since this happened to me anyway – it seems to bring on the same attacks of panic I felt on ecstasy. So maybe dealing with the damage done by cannabis would help the ecstasy poisoning.'

'That's my reasoning exactly.'

Having reassured me that as a homeopathic remedy, the homeopathic THC, rather than making me stoned, would in fact un-stone me, he gave me a prescription.

I took my first dose that day and continued with it for two months. I knew that if it worked, it would take several weeks to show any effects. In the meantime, I still needed succour.

I had tried all the conventional professionals. None had explained away the cosmic contents of this nightmare to my satisfaction. It was time to go straight to the kind of expert who would hopefully believe in my fear of hell. Better still, someone who could confirm to me if I had indeed lost all redemption, tumbled too far down the abyss for rescue.

I found her in 'What's On in Oxford', a cosy pamphlet distributed around the safe havens of North Oxford and the university. A 'channeller' called Alison. I knew enough from the Indo-spiritual books my sister Miriam had in her room that this was a clairvoyant, a person who could know 'the other side'. At this time there was no doubt in my mind that the other side existed. The smack of hell I had experienced in that moment in Ivy Street had left me unable to convince myself otherwise. My remaining hope, my desperation, led to a very serious trip out to the channeller's home in the Oxfordshire countryside.

Marc and I asked my mother to drive us out there on the pretext of doing something normal and soon the two of us arrived in the little village. While Marc pondered his own problems in the adjacent field, I was politely ushered into the psychic's modern cottage. To my surprise the woman appeared credible. Far from presenting herself in hippie apparel, she was smartly dressed in formal trousers and a cashmere sweater. Her face was clean, her curly red hair swept back into a ponytail.

'Hello, Olivia, isn't it?' she said. 'Come in, come in and take a seat here on the couch.'

When we had settled ourselves I found my heart beating harder and harder with apprehension.

'So what can I do for you?' Alison asked briskly.

The intense, surreal situation was unsettling. I listened to myself telling Alison the whole story. As I mentioned the Ivy Street night some of those panic feelings clenched around my heart and my heart started drumming. Alison mm'd and ahh'd sympathetically.

'Are you feeling those feelings right now?' she asked.

Oh lord, she must be psychic. 'Yes,' I admitted, balancing on a pinpoint.

She clucked and I started to feel relief: this woman had at least not taken one look at me and flinched, nor heard my voice and broken in with warning of my doom. The truth about my soul could not be as bad as I feared.

'Come and lie down on the healing table, I'm going to perform some Reiki on you,' the channeller said.

As I lay on the table, Alison told me I had been an Aborigine in most of my past lives and that I could also find healing from someone playing a didgeridoo at my feet. My soul was gold, a kind of gold that was too refined for this world. In fact my spirit was from the planet Plaides. Plaidean souls, who were of an evolved moral fibre, had been incarnated in our world since the 1960s, in order to bring love and harmony to the planet. On earth we suffered a rough passage, since we were, as my experience demonstrated, too sensitive for its crudity. This kind of soul could not be fooled by the addled form of love felt on drugs. It sensed that e-love was not real love, but a 2D emoticon. The colour emerald was also an important colour for me and one that, if visualized, could help my recovery.

I could not feel any effect from the Reiki, but I drank in her words.

We sat back down on the sofa and I told her more of my story and my fear I would never be myself again. She assured me I would no longer be depressed in six months' time. Only half-believing, I felt fleeting relief.

I rejoined Marc in the field, and we walked back and forth across it. His mellow nature soothed me as always. Marc suffered from depression himself, yet he was unfailingly abreast of it, able to accept it peacefully. He believed me when I spoke of my battles with evil. He would placidly laugh, sigh and say, 'Ja, that's the way life is.' Then he would ask me in a serious voice if I had ever heard this particular Crosby, Stills, Nash & Young song, and I would draw him as we listened to it. His calm example made my own terror seem normal and redeemable.

We had to hitchhike back to Oxford that day. It did not take us long to find a lift, in a small smart car whose businessman driver was playing a recent R. Kelly hit. As Marc made conversation with the executive, I listened to the facile rhymes with mounting alienation: 'I believe I can fly, I believe I can touch the sky . . . ' The normal world seemed so far removed. I could never be a part of it again. But maybe it was all right – maybe I was from Plaides.

I telephoned Grace, to see if I could salvage our old friendship. We had been close ever since we had been assigned to sit together on our first day at secondary school and I had noticed that every single item in her pencil case was neatly labelled with 'This Is The Property Of Grace Daisy Mortimer'. She was the most efficient person I had ever met. I had had a mortifying nosebleed within my first hour of high school (they seemed to occur in stressful situations) and she had put up her hand to ask if she could be excused to take me to the nurse, saving me from bleeding into humiliation in front of my new class.

Now, when we spoke on the phone, I apologized for the distant and unfriendly way I had behaved when she had come to South Africa to visit me. She understood how depressed I had been, particularly at the time she had arrived, and was also keen to remain friends. South Africa had liberated her, just as it had excited me aged fifteen. Grace, the lonely, stifled sixteen-year-old who had barely greeted me in the newsagent on my return from Cape Town three years before, was now a free spirit. She had a new taste for travel, the seedy, rough edge of music concerts and meeting crazy strangers.

'Let's go out,' she said one night, and Marc and I followed. We went to The Old School House, the Turf and the Turl.

'Anita Atkins is having a party at Wadham,' Grace suddenly announced, blind drunk. 'Let's go! Let's go!'

At school, Anita had been largely ignored by the staff. They had taken one look at her snapped-pencil, illegible dyslexic script and relegated her to 'division three' across the board. This was in the early 1990s, before dyslexics started suing Education Authorities for educational negligence. But now it transpired that Anita Atkins had proved Oxford Girls' School wrong. She had won a place at Wadham College, Oxford, reading Politics, Philosophy and Economics.

Excitedly, Grace, Marc and I echoed our way around the quad and climbed the steps to Anita's room. From behind her closed door we could hear no music, only voices raised in drunken discussion. We knocked and waited.

When Anita opened the door, I remembered why she had been a loner throughout high school. Her doughy face was still puffed in a defensive snarl, and her voice was the same as always, rambunctiously unwelcoming as she boomed, 'Oh, you've arrived, have you? Huh!'

With that, she galumphed to the other side of the room. 'Now, Tom, you'll be wanting some whiskey.'

I remembered with shame how I, like the other girls in our school days, had flinched to the wall in corridors rather than brush past Anita's obese frame and coarse mullet. It was as if we had feared her butch heftiness might rub off onto us. We had been bitches.

Guilt now replacing thrill-seeking, I followed her, introduced Marc and asked how she was. While we stood there breaking the ice, adults at last, I heard a screeching sound coming from behind us. We all turned.

It was Grace. She had donned a blue cagoule, a tiara and a pair of fairy wings, and was spinning and gliding hysterically from one side of the room to the other, singing 'Somewhere Over the Rainbow' in a reedy voice.

Marc reached for his camera and took some photos, laughing. But Anita was not happy.

She strode across the room and, taking hold of Grace firmly, one hand under each armpit, manhandled her out of the door. Marc and I followed protesting weakly. But it seemed Anita would not let Grace go until she had got her out into the quad. In the clear March air, Anita shook Grace, barking, 'Shut it!'

Grace's twinkling eyes lolled and her body bent in Anita's grip, smiling limply as a doll. She could not stop laughing.

'Shut the fuck up,' Anita repeated, her voice more purposeful than angry, as if trying to help.

Turning to Marc and I she railed, 'Do something, you two.'

'She's drunk,' I ventured. 'She's fine really.' I tried to prise Anita's arms off Grace, but they were glued on like limpets.

Grace's torso rolled to and fro as Anita continued to shake her.

'Do you want a slap?' Anita blasted ferociously at the body in her arms.

Marc ripped Grace away from her and she sank to rest on the grass, still giggling.

Anita grinned tersely, briskly brushed her hands and said, 'I just don't like to see her drunk as a skunk like that. She'll be all right now. Take her home. Bye.' With that, she waved and clumped back up the stairs to the party. I never told her about my dreams. That was the last time I saw her.

After a month at home, I was ready to return to my life in Cape Town, having missed Lennon intensely. Grace and I went to London for a day and bought hair dye and make-up, then back at my house we pretended to be punk stars and dyed my hair pink listening to Hole at top volume. Despite the ostensible fun, I was aching with depression and found it hard even to speak. I had not found the answers I was looking for at home. I left Marc touring England and returned to stay with his parents back in the southern suburbs of the Cape of Good Hope.

Part Three

Chapter Seven

It was April when I returned to Cape Town, and a month passed with no improvement. I stayed in Marc's room at his parents' house and found a job as a 'waitron' at a busy new health-food restaurant in Obs. The owners were a hard-nosed Dutch couple, and the manager was Heidi, an aggressive Afrikaner aromatherapist-in-training. They hired a string of chefs, who were regularly fired for being anything from unable to cook to not sufficiently subservient to religious fanatics. Despite its liberal ethos, the reality of the operation was a strictly segregated business with whites as *bas* and blacks slaving in the kitchen. Each night was a typical scene of the New South Africa. Rich, liberal families and students of mainly European descent sat drinking smoothies, which equally rich, patchwork-skirted waitrons whipped up to the ethnic, hippie bells of Deep Forest or Jethro Tull. Peter, the owner's husband, would sit at the bar bitching to Heidi, smoking, ordering endless Amstells, and requesting Wham. Once in a while, Heidi would go into the kitchen, smile, tap her foot impatiently and tell fifty-year-old Nolundi to hurry the washing up, or to fry her a steak. At 1 a.m., the end of her shift, Nolundi had to make the long journey back to Gugulethu. It was a shock to discover how little she was paid, and to hear Heidi sneer about her. I gave the kitchen staff the difference from my wages.

The demands of concentration while taking orders frequently forced my mind off my doom-laden thoughts, but sometimes my mind would win and I would be unable to work for worrying that I was going to hell or was afraid of love. I would sequester myself in the ladies' until I had found a solution. Counter-productively, on its wall was taped a copy of Desiderata: 'Go Placidly Amid The Noise and Haste.' It ended: 'Strive to be happy'. This depressed me; to strive for happiness was the one thing I could not do. My problem was mine alone. My evenings were spent mostly alone, worrying my way through these problems. I found a book in the living room about the near-death experience, which contained a chapter on people who had gone to hell. They gorily described finding themselves in a pit of naked souls, wandering lost through frozen wastes. Was this to be my fate, since I could not reach for heaven? The depression seemed never-ending. I had no idea if it would ever lessen. What was I going to do?

Then one late autumn day in May, quite suddenly, everything changed. I went alone to the Indian Ocean beach at Fish Hoek to walk and read, anticipating no pleasure, but merely time to fill. Looking out at the sea, I suddenly felt relaxed and was not afraid of it. It was the first interval of unfettered relaxation since I had sucked my last ecstasy tablet in early December. This free, unafraid feeling was of the mildest order. Anything stronger and I would have become nervous. It then simply drifted away and I returned home on the train, to my book, Walkman, supper with Marc's parents and a bath – my normal routine, all of it once again shaky and low, but perhaps with some edge of morbidity removed.

The next evening I was at Lennon's house preparing for my late shift at the restaurant. I picked up a bottle of benzoin oil and thought how nice it smelled, so I put a few drops in my bath. Then I selected an outfit and put my hair up. Again, out of nowhere, I felt safe. There was a simple pleasure in getting ready to go out, in the colours and scents around me. When I arrived at work, Heidi said, 'You look well.' The ability to feel pleasure was stronger than at the beach, and *I* was stronger. That evening was cosy and contented in the way tears comfort you when you are sad. Fears still filled my head but no longer possessed me like demons. I had my spirit back.

At this fragile early stage of recovery, I still had no solid explanation for what had happened to me. I only knew that my depressed perceptions had been wrong, or at the very least, not the only truth. This mote of safety I now knew I was capable of feeling transcended all the peril.

Over the weeks and months that followed, this sense of fundamental security continued. I was still depressed and constantly worrying, but I had a grain of calm. This shred of spirit conjured up a stable world. I acclimatized gently to normal life. I still could not listen to rave music without my heart starting to pound, but grew used to happy folk music with lyrics about love, began to draw and learn about aromatherapy. Only the purest, mildest pleasures felt safe, but that pleasure was real. Microscopic situations filled me with a deeper satisfaction than ever before in my life. Simply putting clothes in the washing machine without worrying if I was going to hell was bliss. Waiting tables without having to pop to the toilets to stress over a passing rush of unstoppable happiness was a quiet heaven. Looking at the sea, I sensed beauty instead of malevolence.

My sessions with Christina naturally ended one day in June when I had no dread to speak of and instead drew her for an hour. Although she had understood nothing of ecstasy, she had created a safe enclosure for my cosmic peril that had supported me throughout the experience.

It was not clear why I had suddenly recovered. Perhaps the homeopathic remedy of THC had worked, or perhaps my depression really had burnt itself out at six months, as the Groote Schuur psychiatrist and the Oxford channeller had predicted. I tried smoking cannabis again, and although I was still hectic with nerves the first few times, there were no more panic attacks and there was a renewed enjoyment. I had to be gentle though. I could not cope with too much, or I became overwhelmed. Music and sight simultaneously while stoned flooded my senses, so I smoked with my eyes closed.

The trance songs playing on my Walkman made my strides through Cape Town city centre transcendent and purposeful, as if I were connected to the buzz of dance. By August, I was listening to dance music again, although I was still disturbed by its harsh lyrics and robotic sound. I wondered how this could be the music of love, if e was love? This question could be answered in a number of ways, I thought. I might only find the music ugly because I was seeing ecstasy and ecstasy-music through a veil of depressed perception. Or, as I feared, ecstasy was love and love was false in the same way this music was false. It all mattered so much to me because I could take nothing for granted. When I could not answer this kind of question satisfactorily I could not love. I became a clockwork girl whose function depended on a series of logical equations. My whole make-up was under constant bombardment from similar thoughts. It did not occur to me until years later that ecstasy might not be true love – that it might bring on only one kind of love accompanied by many flaws and ugly sides.

In September I had to return to England to begin university, to study English Literature at Cambridge. Lizle, Cara, Ann 'n' Jen, Alice, Marc, Elizabeth, Lennon – all my friends came to my going-away party. Ann 'n' Jen had become hardcore ravers. The flower farm was now the venue of a rave empire, a place where every month hundreds of 'Children of the Rainbow' would drive from the city. I now found the girls intimidatingly cool and druggie.

Back in England, that first term, I was more vulnerable than I let any of my new friends or tutors see. On the outside, I appeared an inexperienced, over-protected girl. I often dressed in folkish headscarves and patchwork flares, but I could easily put on a nice blouse and skirt and play a good Jewish girl. The boys I met at university assumed I had never smoked a joint. No-one there knew anything about my past depression, although I was probably one of those yawn-inducing freshers whose disquisitions on their life-expanding gap years drive those straight from school to distraction. I privately thought my journey to hell and back made me more mature than any-one who seemed normal. I respected and made friends with anyone who was unconventional, gay, depressed, hippy-ish, or just plain interesting. There were surprisingly few people like this between the twin Cambridge peaks of wannabe corporate types and people who never left their rooms. If I could have looked into the future at that point and seen myself in a few years time going out with a Tory accountant, as I later did, I would never have believed it. As the years went by and the influence of my raver/hippy life receded into memory, I grew out of this militant disgust at the students whose sole aspiration, it appeared to me, was to become management consultants or bankers, and even made one or two friends among them. Still, in that first year I found a few people who were unconventional enough to tell a little of what I had experienced.

The first term passed uneventfully, and I seemed back on the path to normality. I was well enough to behave and react with equanimity to everything that term threw at me. Inside, my thoughts were still melancholic, with venose tendrils of worry constantly sprouting between any untended edges of the homemade concrete paving stones of calm I was constructing. I had to cope by inventing a rigid system in which I repeated certain mantra-like 'solutions' at the needling voices of worry. I also consciously tried to forget how it felt to be seriously depressed and anxious. The solutions themselves I also deliberately and successfully forgot. When now I try to un-turn what built those stones, I feel how tightly the cement of resolution was stuck. At the time, I was always fearful I might unsettle those stones. My inward life was precarious and dangerous. I had not yet developed a real solution, only habitual, abracadabra phrases that 'turned the key' to my wasteland prison. My basic solution was to tell myself that my depressed view of happiness and ecstasy bore no relation to real happiness and real ecstasy. This later passed into my unconscious, but that term I was still trying to drum it in. It required constant repetition.

The one thing I knew for sure was the one thing on which the rest of the world wanted to rely. My depression had shown me the positive nature of the world. I knew this because the impossibility of escaping goodness had been my torture. The more I had tried to live without love, the more love had run after me, sublime. It was a cruel gift given to me by depression: total faith in the one thing everyone wanted to believe, since it was the one thing I and I alone did not want. I knew that love was the natural state of the universe, and that life instinctively reached for positive over negative, was bent and swayed towards happiness. I knew that social insecurity was a tragic blindness to the ultimate loved security that enfolds all life. In that first term at university, I was at least free of such insecurities. Once self-consciousness had controlled my every social interaction; now I had learnt from depression that the fear of not being liked was a mere shadow, had no ultimate validity, since we were all loved by God and, potentially, deep down, by one another. I knew that people were walking around in an illusion of war, brutality and insecurity, beneath which was the unimpeachable veracity of love. All they had to do was seek freely, and they would find.

Like many other mentally disordered students, I worked as a volunteer at the Cambridge counselling service. We received calls and drop-in visits not only from students, but from lecturers and random lost souls all over the country. There were several callers whom we knew as regulars. One of these we called 'Silent'. He had been telephoning us for at least five years, several times each week. On each occasion, he would not say a word, simply weep for up to half an hour, then hang up. We would always try to comfort him and talk to him, but nobody ever got far. The first time I answered the phone to his hopeless sobs, I let him cry for ten minutes, saying, 'It's all right . . . you can cry . . . it's ok . . . ' I then started to try to soothe him by telling him that I knew he was really loved and was not alone and that everything really, truly, absolutely, was all right. He began to talk to me, asking if I really believed that, and why. I did not go into how I had come to this knowledge, but the strength of my belief seemed to convince him. We talked for an hour. He told me at the end of the conversation that I had been the only person who had ever made him believe he was not actually alone, and that he was loved by God. After that he asked for me whenever he called. I envied him, having such a soluble problem.

That Christmas, I returned to Cape Town. By the time the plane landed, I was overwhelmed with excitement – and so was everyone else. As we touched African soil, the cabin erupted into a spontaneous cheer as all around me Capetonians punched the air, shouting 'Yis! Yis! We're home!' As ever, the moment of stepping off the plane, Heathrow's frozen grey December and aching yellow lights still strong in the mind, gave a thrilling *coup de grâce* to the journey. At that time, passengers descended from the plane straight into the out-doors, onto an uncovered stairway and then a few short steps later onto the sun-baked tarmac to walk to Customs. I had been taught by my patriotic parents from a young age to relish that moment of stepping out of the cabin from an English winter night into the luminescent balmy African summer morning.

Lennon and I spent a wonderful time travelling up South Africa's coast as far as Durban. I had missed him badly during my first term, and seeing him again was paradise. It was the happiest I had felt since before I got depressed. I felt so stable that I started smoking grass regularly again. It was hard not to with Lennon smoking at least three pure weed spliffs a day, and often more than six. I knew getting stoned was risky, considering the way it could bring to the fore any repressed fears. Yet I also knew that while smoking had done this to me several times, it always wore off. Besides, I was enjoying the spliffs. We smoked freshly harvested Transkei with Xhosa villagers in a hut in the hills of Coffee Bay. One of the girls crafted me a necklace and bracelet of baby shells. I lay it by my bed at night and fantasized I was a poor girl with no possessions but shell jewellery. We smoked in an outdoor shower lit by candles during a steamy tropical storm near Umtata. We smoked before visiting the ancient caves of Oudtshoorn and marvelled at the spectacular natural chambers and sculptures within the mountains. We smoked in the car park of a surreal shopping centre, Green Acres, in the dead-seeming city of Port Elizabeth, then explored its toy shops. We smoked naked on the deserted night-time beach at Bushman's River Mouth, running around in the wild windy sand dunes. It was a stoner road trip par excellence.

Exploring the coast was marvellous. No sadness or anxiety were really there. Just the usual sense of precipitous danger I was now conditioned to feeling, like being at the top of a tower or a mountain and looking down. I read *Paradise Lost* aloud to us both on our long bus journeys and in our guesthouse rooms and on backpackers' stoeps and, especially stoned, it seemed utterly brilliant poetry. It spoke to me of God's beauty and intransigence. Milton's hard, beautiful God, its grandeur both

in character and delineation, reminded me of ecstasy. It was
not the god I wished for in my own mind, a god of gentleness,
subtlety and mercy. Milton's God was not my God. But I
could not see that. I could only see that this god was God.
People worshipped this god. I feared it, just as Milton warns
God is to be feared:

> Dark with excessive bright thy skirts appear,
> Yet dazzle heaven, that brightest Seraphim
> Approach not, but with both wings veil their eyes.

I was treading close to the edge.

Chapter Eight

Back in Cape Town we got 'lekker gerook' (really stoned) and listened to Eurythmics: 'Love love love is a dangerous drug . . . it's savage and it's cruel and it shines like destruction, comes in like a flood and it seems like religion, it's noble and it's brutal, it distorts and deranges. It's guilt edged, glamorous and sleek by design, you know it's jealous by nature, false and unkind, it's hard and restrained and it's totally cool.' Annie Lennox had obviously been to some of the same dark places as me. Her lyrics were disturbing. She knew love could seem hard as well as soft. I could not get enough of her song 'There Must Be An Angel', in which she sings of an orchestra of angels playing with her heart. When I listened to that song I felt my own heart swell with a happiness that filled it to its boundaries. I could feel how close that balloon of joy was to smothering me. Oppressing me. Going from king to ace in one smooth move.

Quite suddenly again, on my last night in Cape Town, due to fly back to England the next morning, depression returned. I do not think, and never did, that it was *caused* by the amount I had been smoking, but I am under no illusion that the cannabis increased my vulnerability.

People who use the drug may understand how, in spite of

my bad drug experiences, cannabis had remained a tool of insight and pleasure (and still does years later). I saw it as a drug of truth, while ecstasy had been a drug of falseness. It was part of normal life, of 'reality', and all that holiday I had felt that my ability to handle that reality showed that I had recovered. I loved smoking. I had always preferred cannabis to alcohol. It would not have crossed my mind to take anything harder, but cannabis was a regular pleasure.

This depression was not without an unconscious prompt – the fact that I had to leave Lennon's loving arms and go home to my lonely thoughts. This was not something the depression seemed to concern on the surface, but the timing of my shift in mood fell exactly at the stroke of preparation for departure. We had been stoned as usual and were lying in bed about to go to sleep. One of those tendrils of worry crossed my mind, nothing unusual. 'What if it's like this? What if . . . ' I must have done a good job at subsequently blocking that worry because I can not remember it now. It must have been along the lines of my being afraid of love and therefore not being able to love or be loved by Lennon, just when I needed to say goodbye to him. What was unusual this time was that instead of being able to deal with it, I could not. It escalated into an unresolved problem, taking up my entire brain function. I could think of nothing else. I started to worry about how I was going home the next day and this was (how ironic) the worst possible time for me to get into a frenzy. Lennon kissed me but I could not focus on the kiss or anything he was saying. I was alone with my mind again. The next day we said our goodbyes and still I was unable to focus, to live fully in that moment, to feel the luxury of accepting my own words of goodbye as safe.

It was an absurd tangle in which I hurt myself by denying myself the capacity to feel love when I most needed it. My mind was desperately trying to resolve the worry so that I could say goodbye and feel the love I wanted to feel. Instead, I was arguing in my head about whether love was a good emotion.

It did not matter that I was clearly in love and simply wanted to love Lennon and miss him and feel how sad it was to part again. That was not apparent to me. All I knew was that I was afraid of love, and that the relief of 'Lennon and I', the thing on which I most depended, was corrupted by that: I could not trust him now. It was a torture with which I was all too familiar. It was something that was always at the back of my mind but which had not actually interfered with it so wrenchingly as now since I was properly depressed.

I worried myself all through the plane journey. Arriving in London that dark, glacial January morning would have been a morose experience at the best of times. It was as always the opposite of arriving in Africa: sandals and sunglasses were reluctantly swapped for heavy coats and gloves that had seemed unthinkable just a few hours earlier; grinning tanned faces paled in the white light, looking oppressed and then resigned. Heathrow's endless indoor tunnels and vile carpets seemed symbolic of the tedious prison of my mind.

During the car ride back to a wan, flimsy Cambridge, I was barely able to speak to my father, which in itself was agony since I knew this was rude and ungrateful to him for driving me. My mind was still furiously intent on unravelling this problem, and I felt myself plunging back down into aloneness. We arrived in the nauseating staleness of the car park below college. My handful of new friends, made twelve weeks earlier, I spotted few and far-between, sitting alone outside the library, or scurrying against the wind up deserted stairwells. College always seemed a solitary pursuit, always had the power to make each student wonder where the hundreds of others were. I imagined it viewed from above, with the ceilings sliced away, blocks of tessellated L-shaped rooms, each locked and containing one lonely student lying on a single bed, waiting for a knock on the door. I unpacked. My possessions seemed tainted. All the products I had bought, everything around me from my new lavender soap to a bag of cookies – all were heavy with depression. The next step was to go in search of people. After half an hour I found a gathering in the room of a distant acquaintance. I managed to smile and talk for a few hours, but could feel the agitation volatile in my mind. Laughter, food and drink wafted through my senses unfelt, unlived. Experience could not go on. Throughout the first week of term, I was lost in thought, finding it increasingly difficult to think of anything to say to people. Nothing was to be allowed to me apart from my own internal polemic: until that dispute was settled, my life could not go on. I had no beliefs or givens on which to live a life. Food went uneaten and lectures and classes were rooms of sound without meaning.

Having read *Paradise Lost* stoned and made no marginal notes, I could not remember any of my literary ideas about it and I could think of nothing to say about the poem except that it was 'very true'. Of course this was hardly the kind of critical approach my supervisor demanded.

I did tell a few people of the onslaught. Despite their kindness, I called my parents one night and explained I was so depressed I needed to go home. My father drove straight up to collect me. It was another miserable journey silenced by my mind's turmoil.

We arrived home late at night to an empty house, my mother being away. My father had to get to work early the next morning. I hadn't been able to eat anything all day but now had some canned tomato soup. I went to bed in my childhood room, which had hardly altered since the day I left school and went to Cape Town almost two years before. Now I was nineteen: too old to call this problem adolescence, surely? My old toy sheep lay on my pillow – I was afraid to touch it now. I was afraid of childhood.

I opened my diary from my e days. I was looking for something specific: the writing I had done on ecstasy. I pored over it, picking out phrases that bothered me. Why had I loved repetitiveness? How could I have rejoiced in feeling stupid? 'Impersonal – part of the wonderful system', I had written on ecstasy. How could I have been happy with that thought? Terrified of my own bedroom and past self, I went downstairs and snuggled up to Dad. He was so calm, so workaday. It reassured me – *this too will pass*. I returned in the end to my own bed and willed myself into the sleep of oblivion.

Starting the next day, a pattern began. I woke at seven, with the bane of every depression, the realization I could sleep and forget no longer. The long day of unmitigated consciousness yawned before me. Simply the memory that I was depressed was enough to bring forth a new day of spiralling worries. Every day I found myself standing on the landing calling for my mother to help me. Having suffered as a young woman from post-natal depression after Miriam's birth, and as a sensitive writer, she felt my suffering keenly. She did everything she could to help me, but the depth of her understanding of the horror in my mind agitated me even more. She would tuck me up in her bed, point to the window and ask me if I was not comforted by the trees and sky. I would reply that it all looked fake and plastic beyond description. Her look of recognition and soft, 'I know, I do recall feeling like that,' chilled me. She would play me gentle Bach, in an effort to remind me of the emotion of 'real, good innocence – not whatever grotesque idea of innocence it is you're afraid of'. But my terror of innocence as something I connected with ecstasy swallowed Bach. My mother and I were so close we were affected too strongly by each other's pain, and we both took each other too seriously. I found my father's unruffled, humorous attitude of equanimity more soothing. As a scientist, he knew rationally that I would recover and that the world would go on. I could wail and gnash my teeth and he would comfort me and then talk about the news headlines as if nothing outrageously bad had happened, as if to say, 'It's really no big deal.' It gave me a safe feeling.

I was living an inability to stop thinking and worrying, unable even to try to relax for a second, since willing away thought was an ecstasy thing to do, and doing anything that reminded me of being on ecstasy made me frantic. It didn't matter that my mind repeatedly became frozen with exhaustion from its incessant gymnastics. It had no option but to continue thinking – jumping through hoops of rationalization as I tried to answer questions.

Ever since my recovery I had plastered together a workable sanity by telling myself that what I had depressively imagined as ecstasy and happiness was, in fact, unhappiness. That therefore, e really was good and godly. That it was simply my depressive perception that had twisted my memories of being high on ecstasy into memories of fake plastic lies. That ecstasy really should be taken seriously. I used this logical explanation as a cement to pour into my mind whenever it began to crack with questions. It is impossible to live as an adult without taking certain values as read: whether good is good, whether bad is bad, whether love is good, whether God is good. I needed something to answer those questions, and had worked out the most rational explanation to justify the skewed perception of my depression and allow me to live again. Yet there was a lack of belief. I had no idea what was really true. I was walking on paper without boards underneath.

Now, true to form, my mind was worrying, stabbing through that paper, creating holes of doubt. It brought out every inconsistency in my blanket version of events, and I had to work unstintingly through every last one from beginning to end. If all my ecstasy highs had indeed been good, in the sense of both enjoyable and virtuous, then why had I seen things as plastic? And why had I felt like a robot when I was dancing? And if ecstasy people were so wonderful and deep and honest, why were they such posers?

These questions, once explored, unravelled my mind. First at university I had lost the ability to concentrate, and now at home, I lay in bed all day every day trying to work it all out. In the meantime I could not carry on. I had nothing; no foundation of beliefs.

My parents were worried and spent as much time with me as they could. My friends and tutors at college telephoned and wrote me cards. I knew I had to resolve this as fast as I could so I could go back.

One day early in February, I sought the advice of the national drugs helpline. I was unsurprised that the advisor with whom I spoke had never before heard of anyone depressed after taking ecstasy. I was used to well-meaning but blank drug advice with only a positive, damage-limitation view of ecstasy, which could make you feel even more alone for having had a problem with the love-drug. I pictured this young man I was pouring my heart out to as a raver himself, out on the town at the weekends, necking pills. The best he could do was refer me to the local drug advisory centre. There, again, I was met with kind but puzzled conversation from the drugs counsellors who had never come across a case like mine. The most they could do was tell me it was 'interesting'.

'Maybe you should seek professional help,' one said.

I thought, 'Surely, that's why I came to you?'

My father drove me back to our quiet wintry house and I returned to bed and threshing it out for myself.

A few days later I was hopeful again that someone else might be able to help, so I made another appointment with Dr Gough, the psychotherapist I had first seen a year before. I knew she was not on my wavelength, but I could not think what else to do. She suggested Prozac. For some reason I did not fear it beyond fear, as I had previously. I still worried that it would be like taking ecstasy again, but was not so scared I would not face the storm. My depression now seemed more tedious than all-destroying. There was a lateral, defiant new spark in me that was determined to get well.

If Prozac would help me stop worrying, that would be a

miracle, but I was also hoping it would be a test to show me what enforced happiness really was and whether it really was so awful it would make me panic. I had not had a panic attack for almost a year now, so my anxiety was not too bad. I had a feeling somewhere, after the last three weeks, that I was still here and surviving and the end of the world, or panic attacks, were not happening. I was miserable, but little things that escaped my mind's guard still brought me pleasure: reading a book, or favourite foods.

I became so desperate for a return to the living that I kept wishing for happiness; that is, to be on the side of happiness and God and love, no matter what they meant or where they fitted into my rationale. I abandoned myself to God, whether God was good or bad or e or not, out of pure faith, so strong was my wish for happiness.

I took my first Prozac pill one icy evening in mid-February. I sat on my bed with the toy sheep wondering if panic would seize me. It didn't. I woke up the next morning craning my brain for symptoms of incipient frenzy, but again – nothing. Wary and on edge, I waited.

After a few days, an overpowering sleepiness crept up and blanketed me in the late afternoons, a known side effect of starting a course of Prozac. My parents would not let me sleep, knowing I would wake up groggy and more depressed. They made me get up and go for walks on Christchurch Meadow.

When the Prozac did begin to have its proper effects, it was a curious feeling. I found it literally impossible to worry for more than a short time about anything. The worry would fizzle across my mind and I would set to work on it, and then a moment later it would drift away into forgetfulness. My mind would move onto something else. Being me, I would then start worrying about that, and again, I would suddenly find that worry floating insignificantly away. If the drug had induced complete forgetfulness and denial of all pain, it would have seemed frightening, but the effects were rather mild despite their surreality. It allowed me to drift, to live and understand that life goes on. It was not real, and that bothered me, but so long as I knew that, I was hardly being blinded. I still felt my problems, yet they did not coil around me anymore. My mind felt primed from its recent exercise regimen. It was time to apply its sharpened logical dissection skills to something worthwhile.

The very fact that I had coped for a few weeks and had not fallen apart entirely, Prozac or no Prozac, created a fundamental trust in myself. I had been to the bottom now, twice, and had found I had a core of optimism and strength that would always be there. One was not an endless black hole. There was an end: hope and faith. The paper-thin rationale had disintegrated, and in its place came the realization that no matter what ecstasy was, I knew goodness existed. I knew a good kind of love existed – it no longer mattered whether or not I had felt that love on ecstasy – it was enough, it simply existed. My understanding of my ecstasy depression became more fluid: I still believed most of my ecstasy highs, especially the first, had been good and full of a kind of love, but others were superficial. Ecstasy was no longer God to me, but it wasn't the devil either. It was a chemical, both good and bad. A goodness and God existed that was in me, nothing to do with ecstasy, and yet encompassed many emotions I had felt on ecstasy. There were flaws and exceptions in everything and yet life went on. The yin-yang symbol seemed to embody my new understanding. Everything and nothing both exist, and within everything is nothing and within nothing is everything. My depression had been a nothing, a world of unreality outside absolutely everything I had ever perceived before – yet it still existed. At the very core of that depression was a hint of faith that would pull me through.

Chapter Nine

Severe, filial face of beauty, like one of Milton's obedient arch-angels. Awful. God, love, e. To be loved with blind faith and definitely feared. It has been this way throughout the ages: this is simply the relationship humans have with that enormous force. This is the way e is – the parallels are exact. The way the e-kids talk, everything about them and their beliefs. They worship a god, not e but the love they say e makes them feel. Note the 'makes'. It's forced, obedient love. You can't fight the love. You have to accept it. Open your heart. Meditate. Don't fight it, love's the way things are, it's the principle that leads the world, the drug's already in your blood. But the rush? I panicked but it's supposed to feel good, everyone says it's the best part: remember how it is, at the club even named after the feeling, Rush. South African voices of impossibly tanned, smooth, beautiful youths: 'Ja, ja, I'm feeling it. Oh, ja. What's that you're saying? I can't think. Oh what a rush. Oh baby.' With the music, 'Into Your Heart', 'Blue Orgasm', 'Just Can't Get Enough', 'I Am Ready', 'Show Some Love', 'Push The Feeling on', 'Naqasaki'. The anthems. Stickers in the toilets with cartoons of bombs going off to symbolize the fuse and explosion of the rush. Why the need to push? Why the violence of a bomb? Everyone thinks it's love and everyone thinks it's the best feeling in the world. But I am afraid of it. They conform in pleasure. Why does conformity feel so good? That feeling says, 'Everything's ok, I accept, I agree, we are all one.' Now they are all one, not just the ravers but everyone who seeks that pleasure and that love – Christians, mothers, teachers, children – they are all one and I do not want to be one with that. I wish so much I could, and I sometimes persuade myself that is the solution. However false and bad it feels to me, whatever my instinct says, I've just got to turn my head in the right direction and beg God to accept me. Surely even if God knows I don't like him/her/it, it's enough that I am willing to place myself in its hands. That's the faith religious people talk about. This is a crisis of faith in goodness. That makes it sound better. As Bunyan wrote, 'I will leap off the ladder even blindfold into eternity, sink or swim, come heaven, come hell; Lord Jesus, if thou wilt catch me, do; if not, I will venture for thy name.' I plead you, God, to let me believe in you; all I have is your name, some vestige of hoping and goodness at my core. How can you be good and bad? You must be good. I must trust my own wish, my own desire to be saved. Despite all my fear and distrust, something good still exists and I will leap off the ladder just like Bunyan into the space I dread.

I returned to university and stopped taking Prozac after just two months, feeling no need for it anymore and preferring to be free of drugs. We were studying John Bunyan, and when I read *Grace Abounding to the Chief of Sinners*, I wished I had discovered it a year earlier. This spiritual autobiography through the eyes of a radical Christian in the 1600s spoke to me of the psychology of depression with more immediacy than any modern self-help book. Like me, he was 'bewitched' by the torture of the 'wicked thought' against which his soul fought. Like any depressive, he was on occasion convinced of his own damnation, and had to consider all the rules of life he knew to guard himself from the 'stings' of doubt. His envy of God's elect during his struggle poured balm on my own envy of all the happy people around me, when I truly believed I was the unluckiest, most lost soul in the world. His tossing between echoes of scripture and instruction seemed so familiar to me from my own mental battles with safe and scary definitions of goodness in constant dialect. His torment concerned emotions of both genuine love and misplaced fear of God, the latter put into his mind by Satan, and he discovered faith ultimately born of this crisis: the desperate desire for goodness is in fact proof of goodness. This longing for goodness, no matter what that goodness is and what it will mean, was exactly the faith I found during my month in Oxford. It is the kind of wild hope you can only experience at base level when there is nothing else to cling to. It is the only way to convince yourself of who you are and to assure yourself that you are safe.

To me, the drug was all too clearly Dionysus, the Greek god of intoxication and ecstasy. When I read Euripides' tragic play, *Bacchae*, I could not help thinking how perfectly it translated into the e-culture of modern times. Ravers were the Bacchae, Euripides' terrifyingly conformist chorus of the god's followers. The Bacchae, like ravers, follow the motto 'Dance is law and all must celebrate ... Ours be the common good, the common way ... Let the clever be clever, Good luck to them. There's another road, another, Leads wide to joy.' They worship the god, dancing blindly to his false and cruel song, persecuting the one man who dares to question their 'mind-lessness', Pentheus, whose name means 'Pain'. Anyone who does not believe in Dionysus and play out his forced revelry is destroyed either by death or exile. The traitorous punishments the god metes out symbolized to me all the deaths and depressions e has caused those who have not reacted to it as they should, that those whom it has rewarded prefer to discount. As the Bacchae say, 'Irreverence, challenge – The end is misery. Accept, and nothing can touch you.' Like ravers who talk about 'burning up' as they rush on e, the Bacchae say they are 'On fire for god'. As ecstasy was to me, so Dionysus is a false, lying god. He leads Agave to murder her son Pentheus by making her believe he is a lion. When she realizes what he has led her to do, 'Harsh truth – its moment strikes.' This truth of family relationships, of real love, of Pentheus' genuine thoughtful questioning, is one for which this god has no concern. He is all superficiality, all dazzling appearances and rhetoric to sway huge crowds, and no mercy. Very public things are frightening, and that is the point of the *Bacchae*. It is the story of the followers of a religion, ecstasy. But is this religion, this PR life, moral?

It was easier, as a student, to take on Bunyan and Milton's religious terminology than that of modern psychology. As I experienced it, the religious dark night of the soul and depressive psychoanalysis were different philosophical systems analysing the same thing. The books I had read on anxiety and depressive illnesses (I devoured all I could get my hands on in my fruitless search for the answer) usually seemed mundane in their understanding. They were often written by therapists with no visceral knowledge of the horror of depression and anxiety. Books written by those who themselves had suffered from 'mental illness' were reassuringly realistic. Of the dozens of personal stories I read, William Styron's *Darkness Visible* seemed to get closest to the pain of the experience. The problem with books by psychologists, on the other hand, was that they did not give credence to the phantoms of the mind (with the exception of Jung, who details his own voyages into symbolic realms). It was the religious writing of Milton and Bunyan and Euripides, with their un-modern, unselfconscious assumption of the existence of massive forces that had the power to destroy, powers of good and evil beyond expression or explanation within and without the mind, that gave me the clearest insight.

I started playing sports and running at the age of nineteen; began to eat a healthier diet. I discovered safe, adult happiness, its balanced, gentle construction. In the energized state after a run, I would realize, 'This is the feeling I was searching for all my teenage years.' The closest I then came to being on ecstasy was the runner's high, usually while listening to trance music on my headphones. Like my ecstasy peaks, the runner's high is a triumphal emotion, the body proudly saying to itself, 'I'm feeling so good.' I would lose myself in a dreamy repetition, a glory of human ability, in which movement is freedom. And, as I accepted with ecstasy, I knew that I would not want this high playing in my mind permanently, that it is incomplete happiness, full of vanity. I liked it for what it is: a predictable chemical high.

After graduating I moved to London, and, in the first few months, aptly listened to house and trance on my personal stereo as I was carried by the rush-hour through the tube . . .

'Don't think about it, just do it . . . do it . . . do it . . . ' The unworldly depression and panic faded into fairly distant memories, and normal, human, striving insecurities about appearance and friendships returned.

By then, I could no longer remember the actual sensation of depression. Before the depression ended, I had thrown away my only diary of the first months, and given to friends the clothes I had been wearing when I took the last pill, such was my aversion to retaining any souvenir of the nightmare. It was only after a gap of several years that I could re-enter that time in my memory.

My dark night of the soul was a search for honest goodness. It was a pursuit of the authentic meaning of goodness, love, happiness and truth, an ethical question in a wilderness of falseness. If my story of my perceptions seems abstract, that is true to the nature of the experience. It felt to me like the quest of Bunyan and his Reformation contemporaries, as they eschewed the rituals and ornaments of the old Church for purified faith. I wanted to know my emotions were spontaneous and of my own volition, not sublimated, not falsely compelled by any drug or a social need to conform. It was vital to trust my own soul when it told me it was happy.

A Sober Prayer

Dear God, dear because you are truly dear to me, not at all because I must please and placate and beg you by calling you dear or by following any convention. My love for you and for all goodness is sincere. For my trust in your goodness to exist, I must know you make no forcing demands of fear and submission from me. I must not feel I have to say 'thank you' to you instead of implicitly feeling it. That is faith in goodness. Politely, I thank you.

No amen.

Epilogue

At the age of twenty-four, six and a half years after the e-
depression struck, and halfway through writing this book, the
experience was a whole in retrospect, a finished story. Yet at
the same time, there was a lack of certainty regarding its
ending. It was a new experience, not only for me, but for
every person I knew or met: while it happened, I did not
discover a single other person who had panic and depression
from ecstasy, and neither did my doctors, therapists or the
authors of the books I owned on drugs. Undoubtedly there
were many in a similar state, but the phenomenon was so un-
researched and un-represented in the media in 1997 that I did
not hear of many comparable stories until years later. In 1998,
I discovered that Mandy, my bubbly e-mentor with the Bambi
eyes and perfect tan, had become so mashed from drugs of all
kinds that she had to be committed to a mental hospital.
This was not the result of ecstasy alone, but I have more
recently encountered three or four others who, as I did, had
mental damage directly from ecstasy, and I have heard and
read of dozens more cases. Many reactions were worse than
mine, in that they lasted longer. If the ferocity of my panic
had lasted, I could not have taken up my place at university

or lived without constant support. I would have lived out my days in a mental hospital, or killed myself to escape the torture.

My Gran died in 1999. Lennon and I broke up when I was twenty-two. He moved to the Far East and became a film editor. I still saw my South African friends whenever they came to England or I went to Cape Town to visit family. Cara became an architect, Lizle an occupational therapist, Marc a teacher, Elizabeth an artist. None of us took another ecstasy pill, wrap of speed, line of cocaine or tab of acid after my breakdown. Lennon, Marc and I were still open to smoking the occasional joint; the others took nothing at all. Grace worked and saved in London, intermittently travelling the world. In her early twenties, Anne had a baby boy and began studying for her Matric exams, while Jen found a 'fairy godmother' who financed her study of graphic design. Anita Atkins tried to commit suicide twice, and spent a period in an Oxford psychiatric unit, before becoming a traffic warden. Mandy came out of the mental hospital and began a degree in business. It was the end of our era of untouchable youth. We never shared again those nights watching the fire on the mountain. I never forgot the enchantment of those times.

Yet as they receded, I became aware that they were rosy only for me. As we grew to know one another better, Lennon and Elizabeth revealed that they had considered me frivolous for seeing their home, Cape Town, as a party venue. For the other members of my circle, fast cars and philosophical discussion had been normal life. We had only been a group in my eyes. In reality, Marc and Elizabeth's relationship had been full of friction, and Cara had been a part-time player, with her own separate drug-free milieu.

One afternoon when I was twenty and on holiday with Lennon in Cape Town, Cousin Bobby telephoned me.

'Hi,' his deep voice resonated, knowingly humorous as usual. 'I've got a question to ask you. In confidence.'

'Fire away,' I replied.

'Do you know where I can get some good e?'

I was stunned. It had never crossed my mind that my professional, fifty-year-old cousin would take illegal drugs. And how could he approach me for pills? He knew what had happened to me. He had looked after me on one of the worst nights of my breakdown.

'Uh, Bobby – you know I actually don't take pills anymore,' I said, trying to keep the shock out of my voice.

'Oh,' he said, sounding disappointed.

'I thought you knew that,' I said.

'Well do you have any friends who do?'

'Bobby, I had no idea you took drugs,' I said.

'Ja . . . I was hoping to score about ten. Lucy and me, we uh, like to turn off our answer-machine the first Saturday of every month and . . . you know . . . share a journey. He he he.'

'Since when?'

'Oh, it's been about a year now. It's a way for us to relax, take time out. And have great, amazing . . . uh . . . ' he tailed off.

I gave Bobby the number of a friend of mine who knew a dealer.

The main legacy of the depression has been a phobia of inadvertently taking ecstasy again, perhaps having my drink spiked or even touching someone who takes ecstasy. Even though I know rationally that the chance of taking ecstasy by mistake is highly unlikely to impossible, my body's trauma is still there. I still cannot sleep easily without an open window, recalling the claustrophobia of my panic attacks. Yet I learnt during my recovery that just as the mind can create its own hell, it can recover from any conditioned fear. No fearful misconception, however habitual and intense, is too great for the mind to conquer, if it must. At the bottom is the sanity of truth, and the more the mind measures destructive thoughts by degrees of agonizing distortion, the more the sufferer should have faith that the mind judges all things from a painless, neutral, truthful perspective. The more obscene the vista, the more the mind revolts against it, even if only by finding it obscene. While the mind can invent anything and live in any realm of its choosing, there are safe realities to which it is always moored. A black hole has a measured existence in space. One still has to eat, drink and sleep. Laughter can surprise one, sooner or later. It is a cliché, but the spirit never dies.

If only I could claim that I did not do any of what I have described, that I am a sane, always happy, never-drugged, young novelist. But I will not try to hide myself by calling this fiction. I really was mentally ill, and although I am now years recovered, I must admit to this taboo when people ask 'what is your book about?'

To tell a stranger of a depression or of drug-taking in your past is to risk being considered anything from odd to unsavoury. The truth of it is hardly something one likes to refer to in a job interview, and on these occasions, it has been easier for me to blur the facts and say something vague and clichéd: 'it's a book about happiness and sadness' or 'it's about a young person's search for meaning in this terrible world!'

There is a relentless rule in our society: to pretend to be happy and to have always been happy.

'Hello, how are you?'

'I'm fine, and you?'

'Oh, I'm fine . . . Gregory left me, but don't you worry, I'll survive.'

'Ah . . . never mind, you'll be fine.'

This rule is necessary. It stops us from making a fuss, it helps us to be strong. It is a particularly western, corporate rule. I once worked for a company where the American call-centre staff were fired if they did not answer the telephone with the exact script: 'Happiness watches, having a great day, hope you are too, how may I help you?'

The problem with the rule is that, while it can help a depressed person to have to put on a brave face, it can equally easily cause that person to feel alienated from 'happy' society. Happiness can come to feel false, a pressure, a conformist brutality. Happiness then ceases to be happiness.

In my depression at the age of eighteen, I became a hater of happiness for this reason. The problem was magnified by the drug ecstasy, which I had devotedly taken about ten times before I suddenly lost my grip on pleasure and became depressed. The drug *made* me happy. In my depressed state I felt I had experienced no free choice in that bliss – and if happiness could be manufactured and forced, how could it be good? In that depression, ecstasy came to represent to me a happiness as sinister as Ronald McDonald's grin. For many months I refused to live by the happiness rule. I did not allow myself to dismiss a single negative thought, so much did I fear the pleasure mechanism of ignoring all that is troublesome in life.

I recovered and found true ecstasy again, my own free, good truth. I realised that the drug ecstasy had little in common with my idea of ecstasy, even if it did mimic the chemistry of natural bliss. I understood that it affected the majority of users differently, bringing only enjoyment. A combination of my depressive nature and the drug had interacted badly in my case.

Yet while writing this book and wishing I could distance it as fiction, I faced again how difficult it is to admit to having undergone depression, to not having always been happy and sane. The 'don't think, never-mind' happiness rule is one that I now no longer find either virtuous or evil. It is a cognitive process that I use in moderation in order to get through life sane. The rule of pretending to lifelong fineness is still present. It is a rule of dishonesty, of pretending to be what you want to be until you become it. It is a rule that makes me wish this could be called fiction, to excuse myself from the shame of unhappiness. But I am going to take a stand and say this is fact: fact that I was mentally ill, the honest truth that bad things do happen, and real that I ultimately found happiness.

The summer I was twenty-four, I was asked by a scientist to speak about this book at a drugs conference in London. For the first time, I met a series of psychologists and health workers who had views on ecstasy's mental effects. Two or three were conducting research on the topic; very few had worked with individuals suffering from ecstasy-induced malaise. The psychologists were stunned that I had not heard of them before. It was difficult to convince them, without seeming rude, that I had never found a single clinician of any kind with any knowledge of ecstasy and mental illness until now. They found it hard to accept that sufferers seeing their doctors or calling a drugs help line, as I had, would find only puzzlement and an inability to understand any drug-related problem other than addiction.

It became clear to me from hearing their views that research on ecstasy-induced madness is still in a primitive state. One camp believed ecstasy damages the brain and the other refuted this in scathing terms. One psychologist believed me when I told them that my depression was caused by ecstasy, telling me of a wave of similar cases; another insisted after asking me a few simple questions that I would have been depressed without the drug. None of them could prove anything and they seemed bitterly estranged.

My own experience clearly supported the thesis that ecstasy can be harmful, and I tried to explain to the sceptics that my depression was chemically induced and alien to the person I know myself to be. I told them that although I obviously had a latent intolerance or over-sensitivity to the drug, and a depressive history, that did not mean that the fact ecstasy affected me so badly was in some way discountable. It remains a drug effect for which we have no definite explanation, and there are many similar cases. It would be helpful to know why some people find ecstasy overpowering and sometimes frightening while others of equally unstable or depressive character derive from it nothing but pleasure. It seemed to me that the sceptics were all too keen to label a minority of sufferers as 'schizophrenic' or 'psychotic' rather than examine the effects of the drug. Smugly blind to any complexity, they seemed blithely to wish to quash what they called 'tabloid' scares about ecstasy and were convinced that the drug was harmless unless the taker was already mad. In their cool manner, they reminded me of the kind of ecstasy taker who is quite mindless and suspicious of anyone who does not conform to their love of the drug. The world to these psychiatrists seemed to be split into sane, normal judges, 'us', and schizophrenic, psychotic, personality-disordered loons, 'them', with no awareness of the grey area between. I was taken aback by their easy definitions of mental illness, when it seemed to me these judges themselves were just as deluded as those they judged. At one point I noticed the professor at the head of this faction, seated next to me as we were about to speak, glancing knowingly at my chewed-up fingernails, which I had bitten down to the quick with pre-speech nerves. Did this confirm that I was mentally ill? Her insistence on her thesis having barely questioned me, and her savage put-downs of anyone who dared disagree with her, were enough to convince me of her own inadequacy.

On the other hand, those who were trying to prove ecstasy's harmful effects also seemed one-sided in their view. I was relieved to find they believed I was a sane, intelligent person who had been poisoned by a drug to which I could have a genetic metabolic intolerance. This fitted with my own question of why the drug had affected me after taking it just a few times in small amounts. They believed that I was predisposed and had suffered depression before, yet also that this did not make my ecstasy experience any less an effect characteristic of the drug, as I instinctively knew it to be. Yet their unwavering insistence that ecstasy causes long-term brain damage to all those who take it in large amounts did not allow for exceptions or the unknown future.

I immediately found myself at the centre of this tug-of-war, and suggested ad-hoc in my speech that the whole issue could be approached in a balanced manner, accepting that in the short term of our vision, ecstasy has good effects on the majority but causes mental problems in a minority. As for its long-term effects, no-one is yet able to comment.

My notion of balance was immediately dismissed by the audience in question time. It became clear that each of the two opposed factions were engaged in a bitter war of rivalry to prove his or her own one-sided theory. There was a palpable sense of unpleasantness, almost of bullying, as the vitriolic cynical sect confidently pooh-poohed the simplistic believers. As I left the conference I was approached by members of both factions, each trying to discredit the other. I had originally hoped that I could find a scientist to write a basic account of the effects of ecstasy on the brain, but it now became clear that this would be not only a futile account, given the lack of evidence on either side, but a political decision that could offend whoever I did not ask. It appeared there was no psychological theory that could bend itself to the experience I had.

A few months later, I came across Fiona Shaw's account of her post-natal depression, *Out of Me*. She assessed her depression as well as the psychiatric treatment she received, which she exposed in all its 'ignorant renditions' as childish arrogance: 'At first I was amused by [its] academic and reductive accounts of human behaviour ... Then ... I was chilled.' She, too, found that only a handful of psychologists and psychiatrists in England are researching difficult problems like post-natal depression and ecstasy depression. As I read her description of her meeting with an emeritus professor who 'expressed himself in a tone of exquisite, unconscious condescension', I recognized the patronizing limitations of psychology as practised at the conference.

My instinctive judgement of my experience was that I underwent a depression caused by ecstasy, as opposed to any other drug or my intrinsically warped mind. This could be an illusion: depression's sense of unreality may have led me to a false assumption that its emotions were not self-generated. I believe that the thread of depression and anxiety that my grandmother, mother, sister and I have all experienced certainly disposed me to reacting to the drug as badly as I did. Perhaps on a chemical level I had lower than normal levels of serotonin, that were all used up by the drug and took six months to replenish. The world that I saw during those six months was, in this case, a world without serotonin and therefore a world without happiness, a world in which all happiness looked miserable and all joy became terror.

My good times on the drug seemed more overwhelming to me than the good times of others were to them. There was, indeed, some kind of hypersensitivity to it. Unlike most ecstasy takers, I could hardly dance on e. My mind was too full and I was not in control of my body, so I either danced the same two steps like a robot or staggered around like a lunatic, but usually after a few minutes had to sit down again, my mind blown. Most people enjoy dancing for hours on the drug, so perhaps this sense of being overcome was stronger than normal in my case. When possibly coupled with some kind of physical allergy to MDMA, this over-sensitivity could have been what made me so susceptible to the drug.

To reduce the mystery of depression and happiness to a purely chemical basis is not a sufficient explanation. To me it seems that chemical impulses in the mind are maps of emotion. Emotions can be simulated and stimulated by drugs, but they are a dimension of their own, and must be addressed as such. Yet I know that if I had not taken ecstasy, I would not have experienced this disaster. It was absolutely and without question a depression that was all about ecstasy. The depression was the unmistakeable character of the drug, inverted. It felt like nothing before or since. I was possessed by a chemical change that flung my mind out of its natural orbit, into a place I am convinced it would not otherwise have gone. I inhabited for over a year, from first rush to final panic, a bizarre moral paradigm of ecstasy and its inverse emotions.

Ecstasy inspires a devotee culture that is unfashionable to question, and it is undeniable that the drug has therapeutic benefits and brings untrammelled happiness to most who take it. I never quite fitted in to that culture; I always questioned it. One can say that I naturally had a particular reagent out of thousands of people that was thrown off balance by ecstasy, that felt its highs and lows ten times stronger than the majority. One can argue that all the beauty and ugliness, goodness and evil I met on my journey were part of me. One can say that I saw something that was really there outside myself, that everything I find in me is present outside me in the universe. Which is responsible, the individual or the environment? Psychologists and trendy fanatics both for and against drugs like to draw a line between sanity and madness, us and them. I cannot believe, as many do, that people who have a bad reaction to a drug uniformly bring it upon themselves, thanks to their own chemical inability to cope or latent depression. While writing this book, I came across other similar tales to my own: healthy, sane, intelligent young people who could not understand what made them depressed after taking ecstasy, while their crazy friends sailed through ten times the amount of pills without problems, and other drugs never had a comparable effect. There is some combination of elements leading to ecstasy depression that has not yet been found or proved. But I know instinctively that ecstasy depression cannot be dismissed by calling all those who suffer from it latent psychotics or schizo-phrenics. My rationale of being afraid of happiness was nothing more than my brain's cunning method of forbidding me pleasure. Yet ecstasy is the love drug – it is the cult of our deepest-held values of love, respect and joy. To debate in depression these values held dear by the drug is to interrogate most of our assumptions about happiness. Ecstasy has rewired the mind of society, users and non-users alike, designing a new paradigm of happiness and despair that affects us all.

MY AGONY AND ECSTASY by ROBBIE WILLIAMS

At 29, with millions of album sales and an £80 million record deal, Robbie Williams is every inch the successful pop star. But in a frank interview he has revealed that he is suffering from depression due to ecstasy use.

For a year he has been taking anti-depressants, which he refers to as 'speed bumps', because they control his condition.

Williams has a long history of alcohol and drug abuse and has had treatment for a cocaine habit.

But he blamed his depression on ecstasy, saying: 'When you take ecstasy, your brain releases an awful amount of serotonin, and it makes you go "great!"

'The serotonin in your head's going "wey, hey, hey, loads of it!", and then you use it all up and your brain's got nothing to bathe in.'

Williams said many would find his angst annoying, considering his life-style. He said: 'People go, "What have you got to be depressed about?" And they're right, I haven't. Depression isn't about "Woe is me, my life is this, that and the other," it's like having the worst flu all day that you just can't kick.'

The singer, who dedicated his song 'Angels' to his drug counsellor mother, spoke about his depression in a Radio 1 interview with Sara Cox. He said of the anti-depressants: 'I won't be on them for the rest of my life but . . . when a kid gets knocked over outside of school, they put speed bumps in. I'm putting speed bumps in before the kid gets knocked over.'

A spokesman said: 'He spoke about these things because he wanted to. He has been friends with Sara Cox for a while and they have a great rapport.' A study at the London Metropolitan University found even occasional ecstasy users suffer levels of depression four times higher than normal.

Research suggests ecstasy releases serotonin from blood cells but that long-term use can deplete supplies.